Praise for 84 *Tips to a Successful Business Startup*, First Edition

"Good, entertaining, and very practical. Aspiring Saudi entrepreneurs should read this carefully!"

—Professor Daniel Isenberg, author of Worthless, Impossible, and Stupid (Harvard, 2013)

"If you are an entrepreneur in Saudi Arabia at any stage of their business, then these 84 cleverly delivered, simple and straight-to-the-point tips, with very relevant real-life examples, are a must read. This will be a health and reality check that your startup or SME is on the right track for success. Khalid has brilliantly managed to deliver his serial entrepreneurial experience in a book that speaks the language of today, with lessons that will last a lifetime."

—H.E. Amro Banaja, CEO of the General Entertainment Authority, Saudi Arabia

"I've long been interested in the thriving business environment in the MENA region.

Khalid Suleimani's book did an amazing job of providing insight into the particular challenges and opportunities of the business community in Saudi Arabia.

The format of the book is ideal for busy business and technology leaders. With quick tips, the book gives easy, actionable ways for startups and companies looking to grow in smart, sustainable ways.

Whether you are starting up a new business, or want to do better business with Saudi Arabia or the Middle East, this book is essential reading. You'll come away with a fuller understanding of the cultural and business nuances to life and business in the region, and you'll thank Suleimani for his efforts."

—Clair-Diaz Ortiz, Manager of Social Innovation at Twitter, Author, voted by Fast Company as one of the Most Creative People on Twitter 2012

"Entrepreneurship is exploding across the MENA region, but new founders and young startups struggle to find guideposts that can direct them. Khalid Suleimani's excellent book admirably fills that void, pulling in global lessons and applying them to the region's context. This is all done in a colorful and fun way, with very practical tips that can benefit business leaders throughout the region. This book will become a standard touchstone as MENA entrepreneurship develops and flourishes."

—William Kerr, Professor of Entrepreneurial Management, Harvard Business School

"In 84 Tips, Khalid Suleimani has created a resourceful yet simple educational tool for our region's young

generation and aspiring entrepreneurs. While distilling the Saudi market's opportunities, challenges, and requirements, it provides entrepreneurs with contextualized, practical advice on the dos and don'ts of venturing enterprises. Going beyond just offering startups advice, Suleimani also relays in-depth local market knowledge and what this means to budding businesses."

—Dr. Khalid Alkhazraji, Former Deputy Minister of Labor in the UAE, Chairman of Al Kawther Investment, LLC

84+1 Tips to a Successful Business Startup

Real Cases and Business Examples

Includes essential tips for
doing business in Saudi Arabia

Khalid Suleimani

Second Edition
ISBN: 978-0-9961055-2-1

To my family

My wonderful mom and dad
My wife, Sahar, and my kids, Tamir, Lina, and Lujain
and
Every entrepreneur dreaming of making it on their own

Contents

Chapter 5: Financing Your Startup 262

Acknowledgment

First, I would like to thank all of the entrepreneurs mentioned in this book, as their hard work has inspired me and provided content for the many examples sprinkled throughout this text. Special thanks goes to Yahya and Kaswara Al-khateeb for sharing their stories in detail.

I would like to thank my lovely wife, Sahar, for her support throughout this project. She helped me by conducting a full review of the book, and gave me great insight on the marketing-related tips. She is my resident marketing guru! I would also like to thank my daughter Lina, who was a great help in cataloging the cartoons.

Finally, I would like to the great cartoonist, Hadi Abu Kassim, who brought my ideas to life in record time and with great creativity, and the Arabic edition publisher Jabal Amman for licensing the cover, and graphics to this edition of the book.

Introduction to Second Edition

When I agreed with my publisher Jabal Amman on translating this book to Arabic, we had no idea the book would be such a success, nor that it would be printed six times in less than four years. It is, with the publisher's testimony, one of the most successful Arabic business books. As this experience encouraged the publisher to print more startup and business books, I enhanced the book several times, added a few tips, and removed and merged others, as business environment changes dictated.

However, something astonishing suddenly happened. Between the years 2013 and 2017 extreme changes struck Saudi Arabia. The change of a king, several cabinet changes, and four heirs to the throne ended with the rise of Prince Mohammed Bin Salman as the new heir to the throne. The prince announced his ambitious Vision 2030 plan only a few months earlier, opening the doors to the winds of change that would change Saudi Arabia forever.

I come from a generation that did not witness a lot of changes, and things remained stagnant for most of our time in the business world.. But suddenly with lightning speed change passed over our heads, and decision makers became just as old if not younger than us, full of energy and determination to change, fast. In fact, changes are too fast for this edition to capture, and I'm sure by the time this edition goes to print more and more tips will become obsolete or resolved.

In this edition, I removed some tips about problems that have been positively addressed by the recent regulation changes, and merged and condensed others. I also reiterated some of the tips that have to do with new investment opportunities that emerged from Vision 2030 and are expected to be a new target for entrepreneurs. I also consolidated all tips related to finance (fourteen tips altogether) into one new chapter and added some new tips in that category. The transition or plateau stage was merged with the growth chapter, while moving all finance-related tips to the new chapter. I figured if you have already plateaued with your business, you probably do not need this book and are just as qualified as I am to write one. Finally, the total number of tips has increased by one, while the number of new tips exceeded ten. The only thing that did not change is the book's title that made it famous: *84!*

Wishing you all a pleasant reading and bright future of entrepreneurship wherever you are, or in the new young Kingdom if you are in Saudi,

Khalid Suleimani
August 2018

Introduction to First Edition

The idea of writing this book first came to me in 2011 as I prepared to leave one of my companies, fourteen years after it was founded. I used to manage it full time, so I had a lot of free time after leaving. I felt I wanted to share part of what I had learned while doing business in Saudi Arabia. However, I did not want to create a book only for Saudi Arabia. It was not until I took a Harvard course last summer with over eighty entrepreneurs from all over the world, that I learned that all startups have similar problems. I realized that if I wrote a book and included examples from my regional experience, many entrepreneurs and businesspeople would still benefit from it, regardless of where they came from.

This book is intended for those who have started or are about to start their own business. The book attempts to give the reader insight into how startups are created, a preview of the problems they face, and some hands-on strategies for resolving these issues. It is therefore full of examples and short business case studies. My goal has been to create a light, quick tip book chock-full of real examples from my own experience, as well as examples from world-acclaimed entrepreneurs such as Thomas Edison, Steve Jobs, Bill Gates, and Mark Zuckerberg, and various Arab and Saudi entrepreneurs I have known. I used these examples to highlight the essence of each tip.

The book was written to be "glocal." I think of myself as a universal citizen and have made a career out of technology transferred from the West to the MENA (Middle East and North Africa) region. This sort of work requires an understanding of cultures on both ends of the earth, and if you can successfully bridge that cultural gap, it can make you money. It certainly has for me. I began the realization of my entrepreneurial dreams while working for Moran Stahl and Boyer (MS&B) in Boulder as a cross-cultural consultant, back in 1993. I helped prospective expats, who were moving to Saudi for work, to understand how to deal with cultural barriers in the Arab world. I received a great commendation letter from the program director, full of positive quotes from my clients, which I have proudly kept until today. (Check a copy of the letter in Appendix A.)

This book was written the way a book in this social media age should be. I have tested it with potential readers and taken their feedback on social media. Almost a year back, I started a Facebook group entitled How to Make It in Saudi Arabia. The success of the group has led me to create my own fan page on Facebook, which has attracted over thirty thousand followers, at the time of this book's publication. All of the tips in this book have been posted on that page and tested for user acceptance. Many of those tips were re-tweeted on Twitter also, and some of the stories I put in the book were posted on my personal blog. I have a few tips on social marketing, and this book was written with those tips in mind.

Around a quarter of the tips in this book are specialized for Saudi Arabia and the MENA region in general, and the Saudi-specific tips have been marked accordingly. Many of these tips will apply similarly elsewhere, in countries where startups are just as difficult to get off the ground. However, a number of the business cases will appeal specifically to those who want to start a business in Saudi Arabia. The country has enjoyed considerable economic growth, while other parts of the world have suffered economic crises in the wake of the 2008 market crash and the decade after. Many entrepreneurs and businesses have turned to Saudi Arabia to expand their markets, or to create startups to benefit from the region's enormous wealth.

So, why eighty-four tips? In 1984, software writing became a hobby of mine, and I started writing "BASIC" code on TRS80, after learning to program in Fortran on an IBM mainframe at school. I began freelancing one year later, helping companies by writing software for them. This experience helped me launch my entrepreneurship career in the software business ten years later. I refer to George Orwell's book *1984* in this book. I had never read his book until I saw Apple's infamous 1984 ad. The ad's punch line was, "On January 24, Apple Computer will introduce Macintosh. And you'll see why 1984 won't be like *1984*." To me, 1984 was a turning point too.

This book is organized into five major chapters, on the topics of discovery, validation, launch, growth, and transition. These are the stages, more or less, that a startup goes through. I have used many of the descriptions from

22

the "Startup Genome Report"[1] to describe the different stages. A business really has to understand these stages and be able to use the right tools for each stage, as the tips suggest. Each section contains a number of tips related to that stage of the startup life cycle. (*Please refer to the infographic in Appendix 5*). Most tips come with a two-paragraph explanation, a real-life example, and a cartoon. The humor is intended to help the reader digest the tip and the example, and not get bored through the reading. The tips in the book are not divided into precisely equal numbers for each stage. More of the tips apply to the earlier stages of startup creation, as the whole book does. The tips are considerably inter-connected, with the result that each tip mentions or refers to another tip. Instead of putting these references in the text of the tip itself, I have included a list of Related Tips at the end of each section.

Finally, I really hope that Saudi startups as well as entrepreneurs moving to the MENA region for work or business find some answers in this book. This is a "rubber hits the road book"—you can find theory reading other books. This book is hands-on and will give you examples of how the theory is applied in the real world, from someone who has learned how to do things the hard way.

Khalid Suleimani
November 2013

---

[1] Marmer, Max et al. "Startup Genome Report," Version 1.1, Compass Blog, March 2011, blog.startupcompass.co.

Chapter 1

The Discovery Stage

This is also known as the "idea" stage. This is the stage where an entrepreneur is still thinking about his venture, trying to identify what he wants to do, and putting the pieces together.

Key Activities: Forming of the founding team, market research and market testing, conducting of customer interviews, determining value proposition, creating minimally viable products, and bringing first mentors and advisors on board.

Funding Type: Financing in this stage comes either from personal funds, limited government and research grants for certain type of ideas, or friends and family. Also, many startup teams join an accelerator or incubator at this stage, which provides an indirect source of funding.

If you want to change the world, "think different"!

The title of this tip is inspired from Apple's infamous commercial, "Think Different," which was released when Steve Jobs came back to run Apple again in 1997. That slogan defined Apple's new direction that changed our world forever.

Many of the world's greatest inventions came from entrepreneurs thinking outside of the box and beyond what the customers asked for. Your customers will only ask for what they already know; it is up to you to "think different" and show customers something they never would have thought of, thus creating a new need and simultaneously filling it.

If great inventions waited for customers to ask for them, then the customers would be the inventors! In the real world, customers ask for improvements to solutions that already exist. They base their requests on what they have at hand. It's not the responsibility of the customer to think outside the box or imagine a new fix for an old problem. That's what inventors do. It's what great entrepreneurs do.

I'm going to give you three examples of great entrepreneurs of our time who delivered a product the customers wanted but never would have thought to ask for. Let's start with a famous quote from Steve Jobs: "You can't just ask customers what they want and then try to give that to them. By the time you get it built, they'll want something new."[2] A lot of people would disagree with him, and bring up the market research I discuss in related tips.

---

[2] Jobs, Steve. " Entrepreneur of the Decade Award." Interview, *Inc. Magazine*, April 1, 1989.

*And, yes, of course it's okay to use market research to assess need—but it is absolutely essential that you think differently when attempting to **fulfill** those needs. Even better, you can use your out-of-the-box thinking to create **new** demands or a **new** need. No one asked Jobs to create the iPad, but the idea was there for years—and was implemented miserably (check out my example in Tip 43).*

The same thing can be said about iPhones, iPods, and even the iCloud. Henry Ford is quoted as saying, "If I had asked people what they wanted, they would have said faster horses." The resonance between Ford's sentiment and the Steve Jobs quote above is obvious. Of course, Henry Ford made cars—fast, affordable cars—and not faster horses. Likewise, Thomas Edison passed on producing a brighter gas lamp, and instead created the light bulb. Although it might have been easy to be dissuaded by the magnitude of the task, or by the massive new infrastructure that had to be put in place for electricity to be functional, he persevered—and it was his invention, not the gas mantle, that lit the world. Just as the light bulb altered infrastructure in cities and countries around the globe, automobiles changed the process of road construction, and the iPad changed the course of personal computing.

 RELATED TIPS: 15, 43

I spent hours on PowerPoints, attending conferences, and winning awards, while others were selling, and now I'm here.

Don't jump to execution before you finish your strategy. You have to make sure you have scrutinized all your business model aspects before launching the business.

A lot of great ideas fail because they were not properly implemented. Having an idea, and then turning it into a website, app, or product, is only half of the story. There is a lot of homework that has to be done before a business can be formed around this idea.

A cornerstone to business building is perfecting the business model. Questions about your customer demographics, customer acquisition, cost of goods, cost of sales, and sales channels are only a few elements that you need to address before turning your idea into a profitable business.

During the events I judge, I come across many young entrepreneurs. They may have an idea that is attractive to them but really makes no business sense. I tell them this: If you don't know how it will sell and make money, something is majorly wrong. Many of them just have a half-baked idea and a business card. I strongly urge them to think about how they are going to sell their product and who they are going to sell it to before going to their workstations again. Recently, someone came to me with the idea of a "social recruitment" portal. However, all he had was a brand and a single web page with very poor functionality. He had less than a hundred users, composed almost exclusively of his friends, and he came and asked me if he should ask for funding. What funding? What are you selling anyway? There was no clear revenue stream and no traction. There was not even a complete design, since he was in the middle of building it, and he had no clear vision of what he wanted to achieve. I advised that he should sit down and really think of how this business could gain traction and how to potentially convert it into revenue, before creating the next prototype.

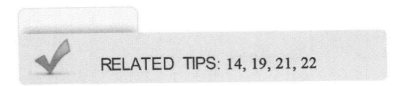

RELATED TIPS: 14, 19, 21, 22

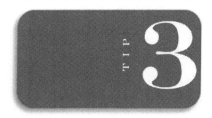

I'm a famous entrepreneur and not a salesman.

An entrepreneur has to sell eventually. He or she will either sell a new product or sell an old product with a new business model.

Entrepreneurship is a form of exploration, similar to space exploration. Both are attempts to uncover unchartered territory. An astronaut, for example, would risk his or her life to explore space before others and come back with information for the benefit of humanity. In a way, an entrepreneur has similar qualities, as they risk their money and effort and future to pursue an idea or to prove an idea that few believe in. However, when he makes it, he makes it big and would probably open untapped markets that he totally dominates. And when he loses, he loses big too.

Steve Blank has a very interesting definition for a startup. He called it "a temporary organization looking for a scalable business model."[3] This definition is very short and precise. First, he did not link startups with small size, as many small businesses are not startups, rather they are simply small business. Second, he called it "temporary" since it is still "looking" for what to sell and has no idea of how it will eventually sell it, until its done with its market validation. Third, he defined its goal as finding the scalable business model that is repeatable, and not a one-time hit. Finally, he defined it as "scalable," and that is one of the most defining attributes of a startup.

Marketing new inventions is probably a good example of selling into new markets. The entrepreneur here is creating a new market for a product or service no one has seen before, as was the case with light bulbs and automobiles in the dawn of the industrial revolution, and PCs and Windows-based OS in the digital revolution. We

---

[3] Steve Blank, *Four Steps to Epiphany*, K&S Ranch, 2013.

are not to forget, however, that not every entrepreneur is an inventor. An inventor may register his invention in his name, but may never get to commercialize it. Most of the time, an entrepreneur comes along, sometimes after a while, as the invention may not be ready for commercialization yet, and commercializes that invention when the market is ready (check Tip 43), like what Jobs did with XEROX GUI and iPads.

One of the best examples, in my personal opinion, on selling existing products in a different way is what Amazon's founder, Princeton computer engineering graduate Jeff Bezos, did. He left an excellent job on Wall Street to create Amazon from his garage. As soon as he learned about the tax exemption for electronic commerce entities that do not have physical offices in certain states, he started thinking about selling goods over the net. So he made a list of items that could be sold, including music media, books, and computer supplies, among others, before finally settling on books. He wrote his feasibility study as he drove his car from Seattle to NY City back in 1994. Today, Bezos is one of the richest people in the world, and Amazon market cap has topped $800 billion in mid-2018, and may increase even more.

The genius of Bezos was not in inventing any new product or service, but in developing a new way of selling books, in addition to all he originally wrote in that list, to almost everything else later. Bezos pioneered e-commerce in its infancy and was successful in making the shipping and delivery of Amazon's goods better than going to bookstores. That caused a disruption in the *bookselling business and caused many bookstores to go out of business. This is similar to what Netflix did to classic video stores when it started mailing videos for $1 in the 1990s. All competitors who failed to adapt to this disruption went out of business too. That is true entrepreneurship that disrupts markets with new realities and takes the lead.*

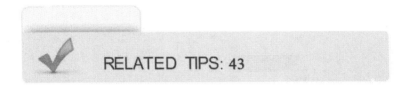

RELATED TIPS: 43

It is true that Gates and Jobs were college dropouts, but that does not mean dropping out of college will make a successful entrepreneur out of you.

Today, with the sophistication and diversity of computer systems, you need knowledge. Computer technology is progressing at a great speed, and a good educational foundation is the only way you can cope with these advances. Sure, you can code your app today and make some money. But you need a whole lot more to create opportunities that will be viable in the long term in this rapidly changing world.

Many of the inspiring articles today seem to focus on the education of the greatest entrepreneurs of our time, such as Bill Gates, Steve Jobs, and Mark Zuckerberg. Some even seem to suggest that dropping out of school is almost an essential attribute of a successful entrepreneur. My own biography shows that I dropped out of the PhD program at CU Boulder to run my second startup. It is true that many of the successful entrepreneurs dropped out of college at one point to become great, but we don't want to send the wrong message here. When Gates, Jobs, Dell, and others started, information technology was new to the general public, and it was still in the process of conversion from being exclusive for business to business (B2B)[4] to being consumer-based or B2C.[5] This opened the door for pioneering. Jobs used a combination of his own genius and the computer knowledge of Wozniak to create the first Apple PC. Even with his brilliance, he needed Wozniak's knowledge to succeed. Zuckerberg, likewise, learned how to program at school. Before you drop out, make sure you have what it takes to succeed—or at least enough knowledge to get you a decent job if you don't.

---

[4] Business to business
[5] Business to consumer

As the chair of the evaluation committee for the Sirb Angel Investor Network earlier on the year (2013), I was evaluating a startup that developed a mobile app and determining whether it was eligible to attend the network's pitching event in front of the group's angel investors. The startup was represented by an entrepreneur who started off by telling us that all the founding team was entirely composed of college dropouts! Now, this might have been a cool piece of information if the company had already made its fame and fortune, or if the team had experienced previous success. But in a situation where I was evaluating the source of this company's struggles, the team's credibility, and whether we should let him present in front of the angel group, that point only served to undermine the entrepreneurial team's credibility. The company was suffering on a number of levels—from a lack of customers, to an unclear business model, to a lack of a clear strategy. Adding to that the team was run by a group of "dropouts," as they styled themselves, did not help. When I asked the presenter why he and his partners had presented themselves in this way, he replied: "I wanted to show our commitment." I advised him to find another catchphrase. Had they been aspiring engineers with some prior achievements, we might have felt some level of confidence that the team would be able to fix the company's problems. Needless to say, we did not approve of them and they lost the chance for the pitch.

RELATED TIPS: 49

This is not begging. It's entrepreneurship.

If you expect to get paid every month, can't handle stress, do not like taking risks, don't have backup money, or do not have someone to guide you in your startup—do not quit your job and go into business.

Many people who want to go into business have their eyes locked on apparent benefits: having a job that they love, working flexible hours, being their own boss, and reaping profits and benefits no other job can offer.

What these people miss is the realization that, in a startup, you typically pay out of your own pocket for a long time before seeing any of the rewards. Every startup requires more than ten hours a day in the beginning, all of them working hours. The founder works weekends, spends sleepless nights, and takes work home every day, every weekend, and every holiday—if they can afford one. The stress levels of running your own business are higher than those of any job.

Launching a startup is like going on safari: it's too dangerous without a guide. You need someone to mentor you as you navigate the difficult terrain of the market. If you have been an employee, your organization has shielded you from many aspects of business that you only come to deal with when you are a business owner. It is very hard to make that shift without mentoring. I remember back in 1994, I saw a piece on CNN about video games. The piece suggested that video game revenues would soon surpass movie revenues. That was news to me at the time. My research led me to determine that I couldn't be a dealer for a platform such as Sony or Nintendo because they already had exclusive dealers in Saudi Arabia, but I could be an exclusive dealer for labels. So I went back to the States and started collecting dealerships for video games, and I got ten dealerships. Top players today, such as Electronic Arts and Ubisoft, were among them. I also dealt with a Canadian company to localize one of their games, and we started printing manuals and labels in Arabic. However, my first shipment was lost at customs—I could not get it out. I had neither the authority nor the ability to clear the shipment. My partner did not either. We almost lost all our cash in that deal. If I had not been stubborn at that age, that could have been the end of my entrepreneurial career. Had I been mentored by a professional, it would have saved me a lot of grief, and a lot of cash as well!

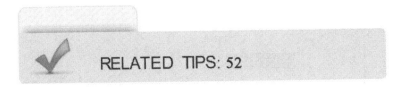

RELATED TIPS: 52

How come 5% gross does not cover salaries?

For entrepreneur wannabes: A $1 million business may pay you less than your current $45K salary.

A lot of entrepreneurs go into business without understanding the whole picture and get dazzled by the sound of millions. If you are starting a small business or a shop, then the average margin you will be making is 10–15%. A turnover of a few hundreds of thousand of dollars may seem tempting for an unsuspecting new entrepreneur, but if that business is doing margins of 15%, then the entrepreneur will only be making few thousand dollars per month on average. So unless your current job gives you a lot less, think again before you jump into a new venture.

True startups usually carry margins up to 100%, and valuations up to fifteen times or more; however, startups of this kind require specific knowledge in a specific area, which is usually high-tech. Also, startups are more likely to fail in the beginning than a normal SME (small to medium enterprise). The formula in the example below provides a very simple guide for understanding what to expect to get paid annually from a normal business with normal margins and multiples. Do the math before you take the plunge into business.

I have known many people who pour their life savings into an SME such as a barbershop, a cafe, a mobile store, or a diner. Turnover in a business like this can reach over $1 million per year, but after taking expenses into account, the owners of such businesses barely make a decent salary. Sometimes, the trouble that comes with customers, municipal inspections, permits, taxes, suppliers, and staff problems make them wonder if this was all worth it. A startup can produce better results if it becomes a hit, but most of the time it's worse than an

SME because it may be something that has never been tested before, and the owner can run into unpredictable problems. If you are presently an employee making a decent living, please do this simple exercise. See how much your annual income is today, and divide by the expected margin of your business. If you have partners, multiply your share by the net margin too, and see if the number pays better than your current salary. If it does not, consider how much of your annual income you are willing to sacrifice.

To put the example in numbers, assume you're currently making $45K per year, and you are intending to partner with others, with a share of 30% in the new venture. Assuming the business clears a net 15% margin, the $1 million business margin of 15% is translated into $150K. This would make your net profit 30% of that, which is $150,000 x 30% = $45,000!![6]

Now, a business with a $1 million turnover is not very small, and even if your business does eventually reach this size, it will probably take you at least a few years to get there. Make sure your business is going to pay you what you anticipate, before you quit your job.

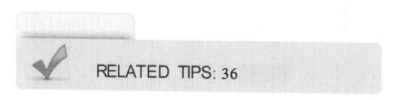

RELATED TIPS: 36

---

[6] Note that a business in Saudi Arabia is required by law to withhold 10% of its income as reserves. Taking that into account would reduce the anticipated income from the venture considerably.

In appreciation of your hard work, we have raised the company capital, diluted your shares, and given your board seat to someone else. Thanks!

In a partnership, the balance of power is the key to continuity: Do not trust anyone blindly, as your friendship, network, and ability has a price and may be sold.

A partner is like a spouse; he has to be trusted in good times and bad. Never forget that strong business associates are only interested in partnering with you in order to make money. If these people are not fair and you are not careful, they may just eat you alive. Having a strong partner certainly opens doors, brings in business, and helps a young startup stand on its feet—but all this powerful assistance does not come without a price.

As I explain in the related tips, it is very important to do a proper background check on your partners before you decide to join with them. Some businessmen have a good reputation, and some are simply troublemakers. A potential partner's power, if coupled with low ethics, can be devastating to a young entrepreneur. Strength need not necessarily be monetary, but may also come in the form of holding the keys to the business. This power has to be offset by the power of capital. A balance of power in the partnership is key to a sustainable business.

If you read about the founding of Facebook in the book The Accidental Billionaires *or watched the movie* The Social Network, *you will understand what I am talking about in this section. The rift that occurred between the founders of Facebook is a great example of a business partnership gone awry. (We don't know for sure if the events as described in the book are entirely true or not, but let's assume for the sake of the example that they are). When Eduardo Saverin signed off his rights and placed his trust in his partner Zuckerberg, he committed the classic blunder of a businessman who has failed to protect himself from the machinations of a stronger partner (or, in this case, a partner that grew stronger). Zuckerberg did not have the money, but he held the keys to the business. In fact, he was the business, at least in its early stages. Because he held the true reins of power in the Facebook enterprise, it was easy for him to dispose of his first angel partner (co-founder) once he got funding from a different source. To him, the value of the angel diminished when he acquired larger funds. The amount of financing Saverin was able to provide was important for only a short period in the venture's life. As the business grew, his role was marginalized, making the partnership unbalanced. Had Saverin had enough money and resources to replace, or marginalize, Zuckerberg, the story of Facebook might have ended differently."*

RELATED TIPS: 17

Vision 2030 is full of creative opportunities. Choose what you can excel in.

In April 2016, the Saudi nation lived a historical moment when Crown Prince Mohammed bin Salman announced the first details of Saudi Vision 2030, a vision that would change Saudi Arabia forever. Since analysts have talked in detail about the vision, I will focus below on what may be of interest to entrepreneurs only.

Vision 2030 promises to deliver its objectives in twelve specific programs called Vision Realization Pillars (VRPs) and focuses on the youth and their role in transforming the Kingdom from depending totally on oil to depending on areas Saudi Arabia has competitive advantages in, such as the "enriching the Hajj and Umra experience program," the "national industrial development and logistics program," the "national transformation program," which has among its goals increasing the contribution of SMEs in the economy; and the "lifestyle improvement program." This last program coordinates the work of three newly created commissions: General Sports Authority (GSA), General Cultural Authority (GCA), and General Entertainment Authority (GEA). From this program alone, hundreds of new opportunities will be incepted. Learning that the GEA provides seed funding for thousands of events clarifies that these events need entrepreneurs to create, promote, and organize them. And that is you, the entrepreneur. Also, the GSA has started issuing licensing for small clubs, which also opens opportunities. (Check the example in Tip 59.)

The lifestyle program will help improve citizens' lifestyles, and hence, it will take care of encouraging investments in entertainment, tourism, culture, and the fine arts. The GEA already has started supporting many entertainment events organized by a new breed of entrepreneurs. These include concerts by local artists and international artists such as American rapper Nelly, theatrical performances both local and international, a concert by the Japanese Orchestra, sponsored by the GCA, a show by Canadian comedian Russel Peters, and a Saudi version of Comic-Con, showcased in Jeddah and attended by hundreds of those interested in comics, to name a few examples. In addition, the GCA hosted hip-hop shows by NY-based Illuminate, which was a mix of dance and a light show,[7] and invited several circuses to perform, including Bellucci Italian Circus.

Several exiting entertainers will now inspire more to follow their lead. Jeddah Comedy Club, which has been active with a low profile for a few years now and is hosted by pioneer standup comedian Yasir Bakr, will now inspire more comedians to have their own shows in other cities. Not to mention popular YouTube channels and programs, some which have made it to mainstream media, such Badr Saleh's Ish Illi, which, after getting over two hundred million views, encouraged popular pan-Arab network MBC to ask Badr to host an Arab version of the US Tonight Show. Other YouTube programs have also secured multimillions of views and are very popular, such as Myrkott's Masamir and Telfaz 11's Timsah, which eventually attracted mainstream advertisers. Telfaz 11 received an investment of $11 million recently in one of

---

[7] "Illuminitate from NY to KSA on Nora Uni Stage," *al-Hayat*, Oct. 1, 2016.

the larges new media investment deals in KSA (Kingdom of Saudi Arabia).[8]

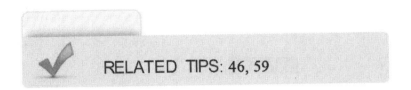

RELATED TIPS: 46, 59

---

[8] Samuel Wendel, Forbes Middle East Staff . "Saudi Arabian Digital Media Firm Telfaz11 Raises $9 Million From Investors," *Forbes middle east*, 29-Apr-2018.

Perhaps food is no
longer the leading entertainment area and the popular national sport in Saudi Arabia, but it still accompanies all other forms of entertainment and will stimulate creative ideas!

It is known to all that the Kingdom of Saudi Arabia is a very conservative country compared to other countries which are characterized by being conservative according to their traditions and applied customs. We find that the majority of the entertainment forms available in these countries are not available in Saudi Arabia.

And despite developments from the GEA recently, as we explained in Tip 8, as the fruits of their labor began to appear at beautiful entertainment activities, it has been noticed that the focus for family or individual picnics remains mainly on food consumption.

All the money that people in other countries spend on entertainment such as cinemas, operas, theater, parks, water trips, surfing, skiing, riding bikes, aerobics, jumping, gliding...etc., we find in Saudi making its way to the consumers' stomach. This is due to the absence of these types of entertainment, and the slow change in people from comfort-loving people under the gift of cold air conditioning and food, to people that love all kinds of outdoor activities. If you're thinking about working commercially in the food industry, the people will most likely eat anything that's offered to them, often not worrying about the quality as much, as they prefer quantity. This is evident in the fact that the first chain of restaurants to be listed in the parallel market (Nmou), is the Redan chain of native restaurants.

Due to factors which are exclusive to the Kingdom of Saudi Arabia, singles and stressed employees do not go to bars after work or on the weekend unlike in other countries. Here, customs, traditions, and other things prevent their presence. However, employees go to shisha cafés, where they can smoke and complain about work and other things (such as their wives) and eat.

Given the fact that each and every entertainment form in Saudi Arabia is linked to eating food, as we mentioned earlier, it is considered the norm in the society. This has led to a higher rate of people with diabetes, which in turn led to the appearance of a lot of restaurants where healthy meals are offered. This was positively reflected in obesity clinics' specialized healthy meal plans, which have become very prosperous and a new destination for business entrepreneurs, thanks to research about obese people, diet food programs, and weight loss. It is important to recognize competition in this market is high, but if you can invent a new idea in the food/fast food industry, or an old idea in a new neighborhood, then you have a chance of great success.

Two girls founded one of the most promising companies for healthy food, The Health Box, and reached sales of 100,000 riyals a month. They grew at a record pace, which made them attractive to investors. No doubt this indicates the popularity of eating healthy, and because of that, many entrepreneurs that offer healthy food have emerged.

The restaurant may not be a fast-growing or a fast-return-on-investment business, but obtaining a franchise for those business products can also lead to rapid growth. In this context, some Saudi businessmen have *expanded their business to become a qualified franchising company locally and internationally. The best example of this success is the Al Baik chain of restaurants, which was presented by CNN as one of the top eight fast-food restaurants in the world.[9]*

This restaurant began with one branch that prepared a fried chicken meal with less fat than Kentucky Fried Chicken (KFC) and then became a great success and became famous. Dozens of branches of Al Baik opened in some cities, that are open almost twenty-four hours a day. It found great appeal with consumers—we always notice crowded lines in front of Al Baik—and the chain of restaurants follows a tight-knit operation, with a unique and uniform food recipe in all its branches. In spite of this, Al Baik has not yet begun granting franchises to others—even though the business ingredients are complete. However, another chicken restaurant, Al Tazij grilled chicken, began to grant franchises to others inside and outside the Kingdom. To increase productivity, the owner of the restaurant designed a special grill developed to be able to grill hundreds of chickens at the same time.

A third example of standard-style restaurants such as the international franchises is KUDU, launched by three young entrepreneurs from Riyadh who left their jobs in the 1990s to set up their first fast-food steakhouse. Today they have more than three hundred branches throughout the Kingdom and the Arabian Gulf. A majority stake was

---

[9] O'Neill, Sean. "8 Foreign Fast-Food Chains Worth a Taste," CNN, September 26, 2011. http://www.cnn.com/2011/09/26/travel/foreign-fast-food-bt/.

acquired at a valuation of more than 2 billion riyals in the year 2015.[10] Finally, several young women focused on establishing businesses based on the preparation of cakes known as cupcakes have made a qualitative leap in demand for their products over several years in the market, which was not accustomed to dealing with such products. While a large group of young men and women began to sell fast food using trucks (food trucks) after being licensed by the municipality recently.

The youth segment is booming in Saudi Arabia, which has prompted many entrepreneurs to conduct experiments in the fast food industry, in which options for traditional restaurants like fūl and tamis shops (Persian bread) and mutabbaq shops (pies stuffed in a special way) have been limited. If the correct research was conducted, these traditional foods could be converted into franchise companies and developed globally, which no one has done so far.

RELATED TIPS: 8

---

[10] Nadia Saleem, David French. "Abraaj Aims to Seal Purchase Soon of Saudi Fast-Food Chain Kudu," Reutters, Oct 21, 2014.

Saudi, and MENA in general, has a youthful population. Addressing their needs gives your startup access to the masses.

The Arab world population recently topped 367 million (5% of the world population), with 85% of that population between the ages of fourteen and twenty-five.[11] Since a great percentage of that population uses the computer via tablets or smartphones, this demographic provides great business possibilities.

Saudi Arabia is known to have the largest viewership of YouTube per capita, the second largest percentage of smartphone users in the Middle East,[12] and the largest number of tweets in MENA (51%). In fact, 29% of the world's tweets come out of Saudi Arabia and the Middle East region.[13] This means that there is a great opportunity to reach this young smart-appliance-savvy generation.

The increasing number of computer users in the young generation has put the Arab region on the world map for computer startups. The example I provide here is from Turkey. Peak Games is the largest and fastest-growing gaming company in the world, focused on the emerging markets in MENA in general, and Turkey in particular. With more than 30 million active players drawn from one of the world's most dynamic gaming markets, Peak Games already ranks as the third largest social gaming company globally. This young company launched

---

[11] United Nations Population Fund. "State of World Population 2011: People and Possibilities in a World of 7 Billion." UNFPA, 2011. www.unfpa.org.

[12] Ayed, Nahlah. "Why Saudi Arabia Is the World's Top YouTube Nation. Partly It's Because of What You Can't Watch at Home." *CBS Newsworld*, April 1, 2013.

[13] Mari, Marcello. " Twitter usage is booming in Saudi Arabia," *Globalwebindex Blog*, March, 2013. https://www.globalwebindex.net/.

in November 2010, and now it has over 11.8 million active gamers daily and has raised $30 million in capital.[14]

Peak is focusing on the whole of the Middle East, not just Turkey. One of its famous acquisitions was the Saudi social game Kammelna. The game is based on the popular Saudi card game Baloot. Kammelna allows the user to join with others via social platforms and play the popular card game. Both of the founding teams, Peak and Kammelna, focused on the young population, and they got what they wanted for now.

Peak Games is moving to break their current highs and hopes to reach 400 million users.

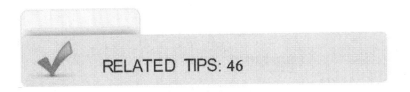

RELATED TIPS: 46

[14] Takahashi, Dean. "Peak Games Dominates Mobile Social Games in the Middle East and Turkey." *Venture Beat*, October, 15, 2013.

The Hajj[15] season has been a business opportunity for centuries, and nothing should stop you from capitalizing on it today.

---

[15] Hajj: Islamic ritual of making a pilgrimage to Mecca at the last lunar month of the year.

Before Saudi Arabia became an oil-producing giant, it survived on Hajj tourism and trade. Ever since Prophet Abraham built the Kaaba in Mecca, pilgrims from all over the world have flocked yearly to Makkah to visit the Kaaba as a religious ritual. When Islam was bestowed on the prophet Mohammed in the seventh century, that ritual was reaffirmed and became the fifth pillar of Islam. Each Muslim has to visit Mecca at least once in his life, if he has the means.

With the world Muslim population reaching 1.8 billion today, and the capacity of the Mecca Grand Mosque increased to three million, the total number of visitors to Mecca per year in the Hajj and Umra (visit) seasons has reached twelve million. So here we are, with a tourism industry of around twelve million visitors per year, from all over the world, and yet very few Saudi entrepreneurs are working in this field. Therefore, it was natural for Vision 2030 to focus on Hajj and Umra as one of its main twelve pillars, with the goal to reach thirty million Visitors per year by 2030.

Traditionally, most Meccans worked in four basic trades, tuwafa *(tourist guides for pilgrims),* seqaya *(providing water),* refada *(catering, in modern terms), and finally* sedana, *a trade exclusive to AlShaibi's of Quraish[16] that has to do with custody of the key to the Kaaba...The Quran Chapter (106) mentions that the Meccans had two trade trips per year in winter and summer. They sold to the Romans, who ruled Syria and used it as a gateway for the import of spices and silk coming with pilgrims from the East*

---

[16] Quraysh is the tribe of prophet Mohammed PBUH.

via Yemen, in exchange for gold and some goods. Hajj trade has diminished in terms of local goods export; however, billions of dollars' worth of goods are still sold to pilgrims every year. The local Hajj industry is under-developed, and as a result, many of them go back home with Chinese products. Local products targeting pilgrims are still below the quality standard of internationally produced products. Vision's 2030 focus on Hajj and Umra industry will open new opportunities for entrepreneurs to innovate given the vision focuses not only on this industry in the traditional sense, but also on introducing technology. Such technology could include things like Pilgrim-tracking systems and crowd-management systems.

A recent inspiring idea that has built on pilgrim tourism is the virtual reality app Mecca Window developed by Visual Experience Co. The app gives users the chance to see the name and history of each site as they hover over it with their smartphones. Other applications provide limited information about the Makkah and Medina holy sites. There are also a few electronic guides designed to replace the paper guides, which have not been redesigned in the past fifty years

RELATED TIPS: 73

Vision 2030 has killed old business models and given rise to e-commerce instead.

Since the announcement of Saudi Vision 2030, it became clear that Saudi Arabia is about to face major and drastic changes. However, these changes came with unprecedented speed and resolve. Many business models, which the business community was used to, became obsolete, and new opportunities opened up for entrepreneurs. The Saudi business community was addicted to imported cheap labor, which flooded the market with low-quality, similar stores populated with this imported help. That era was marked with fierce competition over market share, which drove prices down, but was also smeared by low-quality products and services in the absence of proper licensing bodies that could supervise and enforce quality assurance.

The vision and the new regulations raising foreign laborers' and their families' fees and lifting subsidies from power, water, and fuel pushed black-market visa dealers and illegitimate business to close down. Also, labor-intensive stores will disappear unless they can use properly trained local staff. Thousands of untrained, unlicensed labor will not be able to find work, and many stores providing maintenance and building services in particular will close down or face bankruptcy. So where is the opportunity here? The opportunity lies in the demand that, despite being driven down by the departing foreign workers, will not disappear altogether. So in a typical neighborhood with ten fūl [17] places, five plumbers, four laundries, and eight pharmacies, for example, most businesses will shut down or be transformed by a smart entrepreneur into smarter stores, employing less national labor, earning more money, and using technology to meet demand. This opportunity has opened the doors wide for e-commerce as we will see in the following example.

Entrepreneurs have adapted e-commerce early on, even without the proper logistical support, because they possess the entrepreneurial spirit. Most of the newly popping electronic stores are run by Saudi young men and women. For example, Mango Jazan, Rumman, Baida, and Wardat-Taif have the common trait of exporting agriculture products from remote locations to the rest of the Kingdom and the gulf. We would not have known or been able to enjoy these products if it were not for those boys and girls. While an e-store such as Fyunka sells clothing from local designers online, Avocado sells produce while controlling a full logistical operation, from import, order management, and packing, to final delivery. This lack of logistical support has led other entrepreneurs to seize the opportunity and start companies in this particular field, such as Marsool App, Logistical Services Solution (LSS), and payment agents such as Paytabs. The low number of credit card penetration alternatives such as PayPal is one of the major hindrances to e-commerce. This is about to change with the launch of

---

[17] Fūl is a traditional dish made of specially cooked brown peas.

Sadad II, which allows direct payment online using an ATM card.

While it was hard to believe that you would find Saudis working in a laundry or selling groceries only a few years back, e-commerce made that possible, with less foreign labor and enough income to sustain a good life for the founders. Qlean app collects laundry orders and outsources them to a set of laundries at a competitive price, before returning them back to customers, while Mahara is the Uber for maintenance and handymen. The app includes a rating and payment portal too.

RELATED TIPS: 8

Petrochemicals, Saudi's second largest export, are subsidized and run by professionals. Try to think of a business opportunity in that domain.

One of the things that surprises me is that, even though Saudi Arabia is one of the largest oil producers in the world, very few entrepreneurs think of doing business in that area. Ninety percent of the country's economy depends on oil, yet only a few percent of entrepreneurs invest in oil-related business. Most of them prefer real estate or retail.

The programs that encourage investment in petrochemical projects are numerous. First of all, the SIDF (Saudi Industrial Development Fund) offers loans covering up to seventy-five percent of the cost of a project, interest-free up to twenty years. Second, some industrial complexes, such as Yanbu Industrial, offer free land and subsidize utility costs. Third, you get the petrochemical products cheaper than anywhere else in the world. All that is required of you is the will to do some real business. Petrochemical products lend themselves to hundreds of kinds of developments. All you have to do is ask.

Saudi Arabia has been a producer of petrochemical raw material, which goes into the production of end products, for years. This is the main product of SABIC, the Saudi Arabian Basic Industry Company. These products include plastics, fertilizers, metals, performance chemicals, and chemicals such as olefins, oxygenates, aromatics, chemical intermediates, glycol, industrial gases, and linear alpha olefins. Those products provide the feed for myriad end products. Lately, Saudi Aramco (Arabian American Oil Co) signed a joint venture (SADARA) with DOW Industrial to produce a wide range of performance products, such as polyurethanes (isocyanates, polyether polyols), propylene oxide, propylene glycol, elastomers, linear low-density polyethylene, low-density polyethylene, glycol ethers, and amines.

The application for these products will be in high-growth end markets such as transportation (automotive parts, maintenance fluids), construction (pipes, adhesives and sealants), packaging and containers (food and non-food), consumer goods (foam for furniture and bedding; rigid PU foam insulation for appliances), adhesives and sealants, coatings (a wide range of coatings for industrial, maintenance, and marine applications), oil and gas (pipeline protection and flow assurance, gas treatment), and electrical and electronics (wire and cable, insulation)[18]. The promised margins are in the 30–40% range. All that an entrepreneur has to do is find a niche product to produce. You can start a joint venture with an off-taker (see Tip 79) and get down to business. If you choose to start a plant in certain rural areas, your up to twenty-year interest-free loan from SIDF will reach 75%. The rest can be supplied by commercial banks.

However, the overall disadvantage of petrochemical projects is the relatively large capital required, and therefore an entrepreneur must be a millionaire to start such a project. SABIC has recently developed a program, NUSANID,[19] which aims to support young men and women to enter the petrochemical field. The program includes several packages aimed at

---

[18] http://www.sadara.com
[19] http://lc.sabic.com/ar/nusaned

encouraging young people to make innovations on SABIC patents (as not all inventions with ingenuity are turned into a product as mentioned in the first tip) in addition to facilitating the ease of access for SABIC to purchase products (off-take agreement). These projects are also facilitated by either loans or through investments.

RELATED TIPS: 79

A brand is a promise to your consumer that starts
the moment you develop your product, and has to
be checked throughout the product's lifecycle.

One of the biggest misconceptions many entrepreneurs have is about brand. A brand isn't the logo or the corporate colors and identity. On the contrary, logos, slogans, et cetera are only the outward reflections of your brand. Creating a brand or a promise should happen very early in the product's development cycle, at the ideation and discovery stage.

Building your brand concept should happen very early in your venture. Thinking in terms of branding helps you come to firm grips with the value proposition you are offering your customers before you start indulging in your new programming novelty. If your concept starts out as a school project, you may get good grades for it regardless of whether it sells or not. But in the real world, if your product does not sell, or has no visible potential to, it's really worth very little.

One of the people that understood the concept of the brand very early on was Steve Jobs. His infamous "1984" commercial, inspired by George Orwell's novel 1984, was a manifestation of that understanding. He wanted to demonstrate that Apple was a "rebel" company, out there to change the world. In the commercial, "Big Brother" is giving a speech to gray look-alike crowds who have been "programmed" out of their free will. An unknown colorful character, in Macintosh colors, comes in and breaks the big screen and opens the door to free the gray people. In 1997, when Jobs returned to run Apple, he released another commercial, this time with the slogan "Think different." Jobs believed that Apple was there to break the norms and change the way people think, by introducing products that are different, that were thought of differently, and that would make all of us do things differently. The iPod, iPhone, iBook, iPad, and iCloud revolutionized four different industries: music, phones, books, and computers. That is called the delivery of the brand promise.

 RELATED TIPS: 1, 15

...And what happens to the charcoal if you turn right or left?

When you get your startup idea, start by identifying your customer and their needs. Define your strategy before you get down to execution.

During the discovery stage of a startup, you should do just that: discover. Many entrepreneurs jump right to execution before building a good strategy. I have touched on this same point in many related tips, and I have given it many names, such as "over-excitement," "falling in love with your idea," and catching the "startup bug." But what it really is, is a failure to give your idea enough thought, by jumping to execution without a solid strategy.

The first thing that you, as an entrepreneur, should do, while thinking of how to change the world, is to write a detailed profile of your target customer: age, gender, socio-economic background, and lifestyle. Follow this with a market survey to learn more about the group you are targeting and to understand their preferences and expectations. Use this info to build a business concept and a business model. This model should go hand-in-hand with the product you are developing. When asked why he didn't do a market survey before releasing his Mac, Steve Jobs once answered that consumers don't know what they want until you show it to them. However, unless you are planning a paradigm shift, you should listen to your customers before taking a long road in the wrong direction.

One of the projects we considered at BASEtech, a company that specializes in developing business around innovation, was the creation of a non-violent, or less violent, game that we could sell to kids all over the world. The idea was triggered by hearing how much bad language there was in a popular game my son was playing. I envisioned a game that promoted high moral values that would have parents like me jumping to buy it. I imagined kids playing the game learning polite words and using them, instead of the violent and sometimes obscene language they learn from some games.

Little did I know, until I designed and executed my market survey, how little traction the idea would have among consumers. The idea of doing research on the outset does not appeal to many developers and engineers, but it really is necessary. The results of the survey I conducted were very disappointing. I had not developed the prototype yet, but I was already working on the high-level design of the game, and that turned out to be a big mistake. The survey showed that most parents cared about reducing violence and bad language, but did not want to buy a game that promoted moral values only. They cared about a game that was really fun for their kids. Also, most parents left the ultimate game-buying decisions to their kids, and the survey made it pretty clear that kids would not buy the game, and even if they did, they would not play it. I also explored many other factors in the survey, such as the type of platform, type of popular games, and cost threshold, but what the survey really helped me to do was to identify the weak market demand for a serious game, compared to mainstream games. Further desk research confirmed the poor demand for serious games in my target region and worldwide. The model for serious games was B2B for sponsoring institutions, and less B2C. Since the project was estimated to cost $1 million, you can imagine how important this simple *research, costing less than a few thousand dollars, turned out to be.*

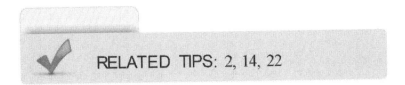

RELATED TIPS: 2, 14, 22

If you want to introduce a product or a service, in the absence of IP[20] or trademark protection, start strong. Otherwise, competitors will copy you, and you will pay the premium for their success alone.

---

[20] Intellectual property protection

Many products and services are absent from certain developing markets, but that does not mean that other businessmen did not think about them; it simply means they do not want to take the risk of an untested business. When entering an existing market, you can easily profile customers, position yourself among competitors, measure project demand, and estimate your market share. Many businessmen see this as a strategy that reduces their risk dramatically. All they have to do is get the consumer familiar with competing products and increase their market share. In this case, the question is not whether demand exists, but the share of that demand they can acquire.

When you open a new market by introducing a product or a service that has not been tested before, you are taking a bigger risk. There is no way to know how consumers will react, unless you test it on them. If you have already done that and you know demand exists, then you have to make sure you are willing to take over a large market share. Opening a single test facility may save you money, but if other businessmen can copy you and get away with it, they will. The only way to prevent other people from co-opting your territory is to make sure you gain as large a market share as you can. You do this by starting off with a strong introduction of your product, gaining customer trust and loyalty, ensuring a great customer experience, and offering a point of difference (POD) that makes it difficult for others to copy your idea. Otherwise, competitors will look at your small shop as a pilot and use it to open up in multiple locations using their muscle in marketing, which you may not be able to match.

In that case, you will have killed your own business, not because laws did not protect you, but because you served a big favor to your strong competitors.

One of the classic examples of market disruption is the introduction of GUI [21] with the Macintosh. Apple did the homework and made the decision to take the big risk of introducing something very different to the market: an operating system based on WIMP (windows, icons, menus, and pointing devices)! The "wimpy" name is no coincidence. Lots of programmers felt that this system was not macho enough for them. They coded in Assembly [22] and called other simpler programming languages, which only programmers knew how to use, "high level." But Apple was targeting consumers, not the programmers and computer professionals who were almost the only computer users at the time. Apple wanted everyone to use the personal computer.

The only problem is, Apple did not protect itself or its idea properly. According to Jobs, Bill Gates, who worked closely with Apple at the time, copied the idea and used it to develop Windows. Gates's rationale for this move was that GUI had not been invented by Apple, but by Xerox Parc.[23] It's true that Apple took the original ideas for the GUI OS from Xerox, but Xerox had been unable to put it into an appealing format at an affordable price. That was Apple's role. Once Apple broke the barrier of doubt and the GUI OS was shown to be successful, it was easy

---

[21] Graphical user interfaces

[22] Assembly is a low-level computer language corresponding to the machine code for the processor being programmed.

[23] Isaacson, Walter. *Steve Jobs.* (New York: Simon and Schuster, 2011), Chapter 16.

for Microsoft to throw its weight behind changing all DOS operating systems to Windows. Ultimately, the Mac served as a pilot for Microsoft Windows, and we all watched Apple change seats from a market leader to a niche player, while Microsoft, backed by the wider-spread IBM PC, became the giant it is today. At the time, Microsoft's turnover was around $30 million, compared to Apple's $1 billion. However, DOS-based PCs were much more widespread and cheaper than the Mac, with multiple manufacturers. IBM, too, eventually lost out in the game against Microsoft, because it did not patent its PC technology. Although everyone would eventually manufacture PCs, they would all use one market-hogging operating system: Microsoft.

RELATED TIPS: 29, 37, 38, 40, 67

Here's a "bonus" in appreciation for your late-night overtime: a nightlight!

Partnership is a very long-term relationship. Make sure that the roles and contributions reflect the share distribution.

It is extremely important in a partnership to identify each partner's role. The role has to be consistent with the share each person receives. If your partner's role is to get you free rent in the first two years, for example, you don't give them 50%, even if office space was the hardest thing to acquire. Just because a partner was nice to you and gave you angel money, you still shouldn't give them more than what that money is worth in equity. Even if the partner gave you the idea and you went along with it, you still shouldn't give them 50% unless they really are going to put enough effort in to match that compensation level. If you have a problem calculating the equity shares, then at least you know you have a problem. Get professional help.

Back in 2013, an entrepreneur came into my office asking for advice; he had just quit his job to start a new fashion business based on a special product line. He had done his homework and identified a market niche for his line. However, his problem was with his partner. The other partner was in it due to his talent. However, he had moved to another country and was not prompt in providing the designs required for the basic line. The entrepreneur, who held the retail experience and the money, was weary of his partner's attitude.

Their partnership was 60/40 in favor of the entrepreneur. However, the "talent" was not doing the job that qualified him to earn his 40%. He was not even a fashion designer, but simply a buyer that had been successful in some major retail chain.

My advice was to rethink this partnership. I warned my client that this problem would grow exponentially with time, and once they pitched in front an investor, it would backfire. The investor will question the founding team's lack of a designer, the cornerstone of a fashion business. Outsourcing the cornerstone function of a business may not be a good idea, and an investor may question why the "talent" is getting 40% while not being fully on board. My client's answer to this point was that the "talent" would earn his share by hooking the entrepreneur up with a relative who was an investor. I advised him to define the "talent's" real long-term contribution to the business and dole out shares based on that assessment. A finder's fee would be more suitable if the partner's major contribution would be finding an investor—an investor who would presumably acquire shares as well, or else a more sophisticated form of conditional shares based on success. Also, 40% seemed to be high for the size of the required investment. This lack of clarity looked to me like a recipe for trouble, with too many tangled conflicts of interests. A partnership has to be clear, with fair equities reflecting contribution.

If one partner's value is short-lived and exists for a limited period, his equity should reflect that. In the likely event this partner pulls away, no one will feel robbed of their rights.

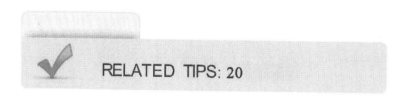

RELATED TIPS: 20

18 TIP

We are tired of being on the cutting edge of technology.

While leading nations from the cutting edge of technological advancement, the developing world is a green field for tested technology.

In the leading nations of the world, there is always a quest to be on the cutting edge of technology and product development. This is not a luxury, but a fact of life, driven by strong competition in every single field. This fierce competition requires businesses to continuously search for tools to maximize profits by reducing costs and increasing efficiency.

The conservative B2B business environment in developing nations, by contrast, gives entrepreneurs in these regions an advantage over those in the West, who must promote untested innovative solutions bearing greater risk. An entrepreneur in the developing world can get away with introducing older technologies that have already been tested in leading nations. This technological lag can serve as a projection tool to help entrepreneurs gauge consumer reaction to these products. Sometimes these older technology products can be purchased for a fraction of their cost as they become obsolete in their seller's country.

In an interview with a popular Arabic newspaper, I once stated: "Technologies require seven to ten years to reach the Arab world."[24] This may have changed for the consumer market, which is now driven by a young population looking for the latest smartphones, tablets, and trending apps, but it is still true for the B2B market. We struggled in IFS Arabia for years educating hard-nosed businessmen to upgrade their old mainframe-based system and use our then-cutting-edge client-server ERP[25]

---

[24]Suleimani, Khalid. Interview with Waleed Alasfar. *Alsharq Alawsat,* March 4, 2004.
[25] Enterprise resource planning

software. This can be frustrating if you are looking to run a company as a tech person, always in search of the latest technology to introduce. But if you are running your company from the perspective of a businessman, it means less pressure and more market intelligence. Think about it like having your own fortune teller, and you will start looking at the market with new eyes, focused on the future. Check out what is happening in the developed world today, and realize that this is where we will be five years down the road. Look at all the time you have to sit back and plan. No pressure from the market to be cutting edge, just from the geek within!

RELATED TIPS: 40, 43

Checking the local culture, rules, and regulations is one of the keys to perfecting your business and revenue models.

This is a very important part of the homework you have to do in order to make sure you have nailed all of your costs. It may seem obvious that selling an app, or a limited number of integrated circuits, for example, does not require anything more than a simple office, and not a shop. But depending on the country you are in, things may turn out differently.

Many countries have outdated regulations that will cost you money if they are not taken into account when you are doing all the thinking and number crunching for your ideas. These regulations may carry costs, taxes, fees, licenses, or all of the above. Any of these legal hoops may mean extra costs or may result in delays in your launch while you fulfill the requirements. You must visit your state, province, or city regulatory bodies and learn about requirements. In some countries, these rules are not clear, and you need to ask someone who has done this before.

In Saudi, municipalities require your startup to have a municipal license, which requires renting an office or shop and having an outdoor sign, even if you are producing an app, running an e-commerce site, or selling nanotechnology hardware unseen by the human eye. Renting a shop and then disposing of it is what most startup do. However, the process of obtaining the license or registration is slow, and it may take up to a year before you can get all the necessary permits., which is a hidden cost that may consume all of the entrepreneur's capital before he or she even starts.[26] Also, what you put in your CR[27] as a work activity can also

---

[26] Check the table in Appendix 3 detailing required costs to start a business in KSA.

[27] CR= Commercial registration

influence the type of workforce you can hire, especially if you intend to get foreign labor and apply for a visa and work permit for those foreign laborers. However, if you intend to work alone, you can apply for the recent freelance license and may not be required to have an office. If you do this, you have to be working alone, and you will not be able to have a CR. This applies to seventy-two professions, including web design and photography.

When I first applied for visas, I could not hire engineers, only technicians, because something I had listed under "type of businesses" in my CR was labeled incorrectly. At the time, there was no "software" classification for a business activity, so I had to put "hardware." That classification cost me time and money, even though we only sold software. We had similar problems with the Department of Zakat[28] and income tax, who thought we were avoiding paying customs, because we had no custom costs. They assumed we were involved in imports, since we were a foreign dealership; in reality, however, we received our "imported" software on DVDs by mail, and later via the Internet. The example included with Tip 21 illustrates another way in which a business might suffer as a result of failing to consider customs costs for imported goods.

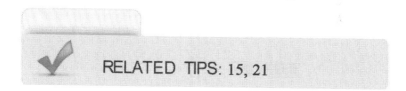

RELATED TIPS: 15, 21

---

[28] Zakat: An Islamic tax on retained income of 2.5% per year.

In a startup, be wary of committing to partnerships you may not be able to shake off later.

A partnership is like a marriage. It is a long-term commitment, where both parties invest in the relationship for the long haul. However, like any marriage, your partnership will one day end, either by divorce or death. In business, a partnership also ends if the terms or purpose of the partnership end.

Make sure that your partner's usefulness does not expire, or that his expiry is timed with the end of the partnership and not before. Some partners are good to have at the outset of a venture, as they serve a certain purpose. But their expertise may expire, may become irrelevant, or may even become a hindrance. Before you reach out your hand and make that long-term commitment to this partner, consider whether you will really need him forever. If not, find another formula that takes into account the expiry of his benefit to the partnership.

Back in the 1990s, when I was new to business, one of my partners was a corporate executive, and I was just a young engineer still attending classes at the graduate school of CU Boulder. I did not know much about business, let alone business in Saudi Arabia. The benefit he brought to our partnership was mediocre financing plus a couple of leads he could provide in the early days of the venture. However, the reason I really needed him was for the infrastructure he provided me, including access to government expeditors, office space, work permits for expats, and many other things I had no clue how to do. With time, however, I learned that those things could be easily acquired. What remained in our partnership was long-term value, which he did not create. The 50/50 partnership we made had seemed fair in the early days, but as time passed, the benefits from that partner diminished, and his share did not seem to fairly reflect his contributions, which diminished over time. At times, he even tried to create fictitious problems so that he could maintain his status as a superior "know-it-all" partner. This may sound ungrateful, but the fact is, this sort of imbalance is the reason why many partnerships end. If one partner's role is to provide services that will help the business in the beginning, then these services should be quantified. If only one of the partners is going to continue working while the other banks on the contributions he provided in the very early days, then maybe an equal partnership will cause problems in the future.

 RELATED TIPS: 17

Don't let overexcitement stop you from doing your homework. Lack of proper research into the elements affecting your startup may spell its end.

One of the key steps in the validation stage is to collect metrics based on your MVP (minimum viable product) and then pivot as necessary. Proper research helps you to adjust your idea before launch to make it as close to perfection as possible. The more you do your homework, the less you will have to make painful late-game adjustments and pivots.

Other factors that may not have to do with the product itself can have a great impact on your business as well. A bad partner or a lack of finances can kill your startup in the "Valley of Death."[29] Bad human resources can hinder your startup or may even steal and sell your idea. Bad advice can be toxic and may delay you to the extent that it stops your launch forever. A bad choice of a first customer can also be devastating to your startup if they abuse you, ask for too much, or spread bad publicity about you. Doing your homework can help you to prevent all of this.

A very enthusiastic entrepreneur from Jordan launched an online business selling goods from China. He had already started selling through Facebook and other social media platforms and had enjoyed considerable growth in traction within the first six months of his business, averaging a 15% increase per month. He recovered most of his capital and was ready to move from validation to growth. Or so he thought. Part of the validation stage is working with the numbers you get out of your soft launch and validating your business model

---

[29] "Valley of Death" is a phrase that describes where most startups fail due to a lack of revenues to sustain the business.

and all of the business aspects. The main problem with this business was that the founders had never put down the numbers and figured out whether they could make profits or not. They were planning on renting a showroom and expanding their business, but after crunching the numbers, it turned out they were already running at a loss, even though they stored the goods at their own homes. They certainly could not afford to rent a warehouse under their current margins.

Their main problem was in the supply chain, payment methods, and distribution. Jordan couriers did not reach all their clients and were expensive. Their goods were discount accessories for teenage girls, and many of their customers did not have credit cards, and paid cash on delivery, so they had a van that went all around Jordan to deliver. One of the major mistakes the business made was neglecting customs costs. This had a negative impact on their bottom line as soon as the first shipment cleared. To increase sales, they needed more vans and drivers to cover the territory. The homework I gave them was to review their supply chain process and try to find a more cost-effective means to deliver the goods to customers. I also asked them to analyze the geographical spread of their customers, and find out which were the easiest to acquire and the most profitable. One solution that might arise from this analysis is a shift to focus on a certain area, which they could continue to serve under their current resources while turning a profit. Once the business model is validated, only then should scaling the business be considered.

This example demonstrates how important it is to launch an MVP, and how important it is to validate the business model based on real data. Validation is the focus of all the tips in the next Chapter.

 RELATED TIPS: 15, 19, 22

Chapter 2
The Validation Stage

In this stage, startups are looking to get early validation of their business model. This is manifested by getting their first set of customers on board, and landing those customers should be the entrepreneur's main focus at this stage. Your ability to gain and retain customers is an indicator of broader interest in your product. Sometimes, this validation is manifested by making sales, or by attracting a large number of users, who can be converted to buyers at a later stage. Leveraging this validation through PR and other marketing activities is crucial to gaining prospective customer trust.

Key Activities: Refinement of core features; customer growth; identification of success metrics; implementation of analytics, followed by pivots if necessary. Also, the first key hires are made, first paying customers may come on board, and product market fit is tested and validated.

Funding Type: Seed funding and grants. Startups get better chances to join accelerators at this stage.

I'm not lost, I'm pivoting.

Most startups adjust their business model more than once until they get it right. Don't worry, pivot!!

Another way to phrase this tip is, "Never fall in love with your idea." Your idea is good only if it sells. In rare cases, you may be ahead of the market and have to take the rough road to educating the market first, but in many other cases, you simply need to adjust your business model, your marketing strategy, or your branding strategy to fit the consumer's taste. In any of those cases, your product is not ready to launch.

The act of making changes to your business model or product has a nice name: They call it "pivoting." Eric Ries, the father of the "lean startup," defines pivoting as "structured course correction designed to test a new fundamental hypothesis about the product, strategy, and engine of growth."[30] Most businesses have to pivot more than once before they reach the optimum combination of product and business. Your product was not bestowed on you, it's not sacred, and no one out there is really going to mock you if you change it up. So go ahead and pivot and re-pivot until you get it right.

Back in 2011, the Kingdom decided to encourage women to work in fashion retail, an area that up until then was being covered by young men from neighboring countries. This opened an opportunity to hire over one million women who had never worked in that business area before. I was approached, as an angel investor, by a fashion professional who wanted to open a training facility. The opportunity was clear. We did some market research that confirmed the obvious: retailers wanted to hire trained

---

[30]Ries, Eric. *The Lean Startup: How Today's Entrepreneurs Use Continuous Innovation to Create Radically Successful Businesses.* (New York: Crown Publishing, 2011), p. 11.

women to sell their products. But as we were getting started, the government introduced a deadline by which all retail stores had to be run by saleswomen only. This pushed retailers to hire any girls, with any background, immediately, and then worry about putting them through some crash internal training program later. This decreased the demand for our service dramatically. We responded by pivoting our business model: we turned the training center into a recruitment agency and offered some additional qualification programs. We knew we would increase training services with time, but for now we had to sell something. That something was recruitment, and it turned out to be successful.

 RELATED TIPS: 15, 28

Saudi support for entrepreneurship is shallow and will not exceed the validation stage by any means.

I started my first business in a period that did not know the term *entrepreneurship*, and getting a job was the hope of most young people. A few decades earlier, when the Kingdom was in its infancy and needed many of its sons to fill government posts and jobs, there was a systematic campaign encouraging young people to engage in government work. In the '50s and '60s and until the '70s of the last century, such campaigns directed the youth to leave the work inherited from their ancestors for thousands of years of free work. My father reminded me that my late grandfather told him that having a job was similar to begging because the employee extends his hand by the end of the month to collect his salary. The people of Mecca, where my father and his father before him were born, had lived for thousands of years as a city of merchants, craftsmen, and entrepreneurs.

After the decline of oil income in the '80s and '90s of the last century, jobs became relatively scarce, but the culture of self-employment had been lost and became degraded for some, and therefore the move from salaried jobs for young people was limited to the transition from the public sector to the private sector, seeking job security from major companies such as SABIC, Aramco, Saudi Telecom, and Saudi Airlines. No way were they to accept entrepreneurial jobs.

However, by the end of the first decade of the new millennium, the State had taken an interest in the importance of educating young people on the importance of entrepreneurship. It launched an intensive campaign to encourage entrepreneurship and self-employment once again. It established the Badir Business Incubator

Program and the Ministry of Labour, established initiatives to influence young people, such as the Israr (Perseverance) Award. It began to mutate into culture until we noticed a lot of people wearing the "entrepreneurship" medal. However, this media attention has led to the emergence of a new class of lovers of the spotlight, fame, and awards. They are what we call "showpreneurs" or "wannapreneurs." (See Tip 81.)

The lack of entrepreneurial support when I started my business has not changed much today despite the media hype and the great encouragement. The Ministry of Labor, the sponsor of the Israr (perseverance) Award, is the biggest rock that breaks the persistence/perseverance of young people, with annoying requests, inspections, and fines that do not differentiate between a young entrepreneur and a veteran businessman. As for the Badir Program, which incubates entrepreneurs and provides them with the offices and saves their expenses, as explained in the relevant advice, their role does not exceed the guidance at the stage of the idea in addition to some minor theoretical guidance. However, the incubator cannot obtain a municipal permit for the startup that's officially incubated by a government agency! Municipalities did not recognize "co-working space" offices until April 2018. Before that, they required a fully furnished office as we shall see in the following example.

In America, when they say, "The party is over," it means that the time for seriousness has begun. The party for entrepreneurs ends when the commercial registration or CR is issued, in 180 seconds, as promoted by the Ministry of Commerce and Investment. However, this CR does not even equal the value of the ink that it was printed with, unless it is accompanied by work permits, which may take 180 days or double that time. The beginning of the activity requires three essential licenses: the license of the municipality, the Ministry of Labor permit, and the registration in social insurance (GOSI) or filing for employees records with the authorities. Without these licenses, the business is considered illegal. To obtain a municipal license, it is necessary to rent a furnished office/shop and obtain the approval of the municipality. However, the delay of the permit for reasons such as failure to complete the requirements of the civil defense department may mean that the entrepreneur loses his capital in rent and furniture without the actual exercise of the activity the office was rented for. We have developed a scenario for the costs of setting up the company and tried to access support, and we found the direct costs to be in the 10,000 riyal range. While the hidden costs, such as rent and furniture that are inevitable to supply until business activities started, were up to the total of nearly 100,000 riyals. (See Appendix 3.) Therefore, an entrepreneur's capital of 100,000 riyals will often be spent to meet government and ministerial requests. These parties do not spot entrepreneurs in their radar, and deal with entrepreneurs like they deal with big traders. Even the only program that supports entrepreneurs, carried out by Hadaf under the Human Resources Development Fund (HRDF), which is a support of 3,000 riyals per month if this is the first CR of business activity, is limited, with difficult requirements, and not for everyone.[31] The Small and Medium Enterprise Authority (SMEA) has announced a program to refund government fees to first-time entreprenuers, and it's a major incentive. However, it only helps in refunding direct costs detailed in Appendix 3, and not the undirect ones.

It should be noted that if the entrepreneur's business is not traditional and requires a license from a third party such as the health, media, or any other ministry, the procedural complexity is multiplied, as well as the investment and the required time. Still and even today, despite the existence of a support SMEA, the licenses remain in the hands of government agencies that have minimum consideration or preference for an entrepreneur over any enterprise whose capital may be in the hundreds of millions.

RELATED TIPS: 64, 69

[31] www.hrdf.com

I'm going to demonstrate my talents before the presentation.

A presentation is the few minutes you are given to pitch your project. Be clear. Investors like those who do their homework, and hate those who beat around the bush.

Businessmen are busy people. They are bombarded daily by hundreds of entrepreneurs offering a partnership or a business deal or requesting financial help. As a result, they are typically very selective of who they want to meet and how much time they want to invest in those people. Getting an appointment is only a first step to getting a potential investor's attention.

Once you get that appointment, you have only a few minutes to make a good impression and grab their attention. Do not waste their time explaining your Cinderella story, how many lines of code you spat, or how technologically superior your product is. To them, all this makes little or no difference. The most important thing is how much money you want, for how much equity, how you will return their money, and for how much profit. Let this be the focus of your presentation; make it quick, short, and to the point. If you get a second appointment, then you can elaborate on other aspects of the business.

During the events I coach and judge, I have noticed that many startups come into the pitch proud of their product and prepared to answer detailed questions about their product features and coding techniques, but get caught off guard when asked the four basic questions: How much money do you want? For how much equity? For what kind of return? And when? When you go and ask for funding, be sure you have had your company valued professionally, and make sure you are clear on what you want and what your investor will want.

In an event organized by Sophia Business Angels of Sophia Antipolis, France, around ten startups from Asia, MENA, Europe, and the US were asked to pitch in front of a panel of multinational judges; I was one of those judges. After the initial session, the entrepreneurs got to listen to our comments and pitch again. Nine out of ten of those entrepreneurs failed to address the above basic questions in their presentations. One startup blew four of their five minutes on their Cinderella story: how they met and how they bought office furniture. They then had to rush through twenty more slides when they got the "one minute left" cue. Of course, this strategy made them lose, even though they probably had the most stable model and the highest growth potential. A similar result will happen for these entrepreneurs again if they do the same thing in front of an investor; situations like this, in which an investor loses interest and never gives the founders a chance for a second demo, can be devastating to a startup's ultimate chances.

 RELATED TIPS: 26, 33

We are a two-founder startup.

Your startup team is one of the key elements an investor looks at. Make sure you cover the primary functions of the business with at least three people.

When pitching for investment, many entrepreneurs choose to go it alone. It might be nice for your ego to show you are the "do-it-all Superman," but that will not seem convincing to your potential investors. Unless you are applying to an incubator or a seed fund, to develop an idea, your investors will be looking for sustainability and a scalable business. This is hard for one "lone ranger" to achieve.

Your founding team should have the skills to cover the basic functions of a business: technical or production, sales and marketing, finance and administration. Two to three people is the absolute minimum. Investors know that once you start making money, you will need more people. They want to see that you are aware of that, you have people that can take the lead on the basic functions, and you are ready to launch a business based on your product or innovation.

In one of the pitching events for Sirb Angel group, an aspiring young cartoonist pitched a cartoon production company. He was talented and had many cute demos of children's animated books and cartoons. But he was not ready to start a company. One of the investors he pitched in front of had the following questions:

-What are you doing now?
>I'm a student.

-Do you plan to do this full time?
>Eventually.

-When do you plan to start full time?
>When I graduate.

-*When you say "we," do you mean anyone else but yourself?*
>No.

-*Is there anyone else helping you to start and run a business?*
>No.

It will come as no surprise that the final verdict was to ask the aspiring cartoonist to come back when he had a real basic structure for a company, had assembled some resources, and was ready for an investment. Three years later I met the entrepreneur, who had graduated and taken the advice to heart. He was incubated by then, had a team of two, registered his company, and secured a number of contracts. I asked him to reapply, and he said he would want to grow his business further before asking for investment. This is a sign of how mature this entrepreneur has become. However, this was just one example of how Sirb Angel's investment policy has borne fruit. In the February 2018 event of Sirb, the performance of the group in the past four years was exhibited. The companies grew by 67%, yielded an average IRR of 96%, and had an ROI of almost threefold on the original investment. Not bad for one of the first angel groups in Saudi Arabia!

RELATED TIPS: 34

You may get away with no business plan when pitching for investment at the early stages of your startup, but you will always need a valuation.

Many seasoned investors and entrepreneurs alike advocate for the "no business plan" plan. This means they encourage entrepreneurs with early-stage startups not to waste time building lengthy business plans. By the time the plan is read, if it ever is, it may be outdated already. This is reasonable advice, due to the fast-changing nature of startups and the fact that all business plans are based on projection and speculations of success in the future. If you do produce a business plan, it can be very short. One of the famous examples is the email the Google founders presented to get an investment from Excite; it was a two-page document only. [32] The founders of Saudi Uturn, mentioned in Tip 46's example, got their first angel investor with no business plan at all.

Even if you can get away with a short or no business plan, however, it's still in your best interests to have an idea of how much you value your startup. Asking for investment means selling equity, and to determine how much value each equity share is worth, you have to have a price for your business; i.e., a valuation. This valuation need not have been done professionally—though many VC[33]s may ask you to do this—but it has to be a number you are ready to negotiate and defend in front of the investor. A lack of preparation puts you at a disadvantage come negotiation time.

Most of the startups that pitch in front of us in judging panels are so excited that they come to the pitch not knowing a rat's tail about how much money they want,

---

[32] Kerr, William. "Business Model Analysis." *Launching New Ventures Notes*, Harvard Business School, June 2013.
[33] Venture capitalists

how much equity the investment will be drawn against, or what their expected internal rate of return (IRR) is. I once asked an entrepreneur who was pitching in front of me: "You are asking for $100K against what equity?"

He was so caught off guard that he asked me to suggest a percentage! As a follow-up question, I asked him, "What is the valuation of your business?" The answer was that he had not valued it yet!! The startup was based on a good idea, but a lack of financial preparation such as this man showed can throw off investors, or provoke opportunists to take advantage of unwary entrepreneurs. Investment in a valuation and simple private placement memorandum (PPM) is worth it if you consider the consequences of being undervalued or taken advantage of by an investor. If you can't afford an expensive valuation, try to have one done by a freelancer, and let them explain to you how to defend the number.

RELATED TIPS: 24, 71, 83

In Saudi Arabia, technically, there is no difference between an expat work permit for a rocket scientist or a janitor.

One of the major problems any entrepreneur faces in Saudi is a lack of resources, whether skilled or labor. Saudis rarely take labor jobs, and yet, even for skilled workers, the demand is higher than the supply. So far, the country's supply of technicians, engineers, bankers, accountants, and lawyers is not enough to meet the demands of the growing economy.

Traditionally, startups have not been attractive to young professionals. These people would rather work for large corporations such as the oil company, the electric company, the airlines, or petrochemical conglomerates. In recent years, a growing number of Saudis have become interested in starting their own businesses, but few are interested in working for others. Therefore, in the absence of local labor, and regardless of tightened restrictions from the Ministry of Labor, often, getting a foreign professional a work permit or a visa is the only way to go. The dilemma is that expats all fall within the same quota. It does not matter if you are bringing in a real asset with advanced knowledge or a laborer with limited or no skills. This does not seem fair to high-tech startups transferring important knowledge that the country needs badly.

We have always been faced with the challenge of attracting talent, since the days of IFS Arabia. At that time, we were implementing cutting-edge software, and we needed highly skilled professionals and engineers from different disciplines for different modules. We needed industrial engineers for manufacturing, accountants for financials, business grads for HR, and so on. It was very hard to find such resources locally, and the people we did find were foreign expats. The fact that we were contributing to the economy by transferring knowledge of an advanced system that helped larger corporations did not make a difference to the Labor Office, the body in charge of issuing foreign work permits. The visa quota did not differentiate between professions and skills. In our quota for foreign expats, even the janitor, the driver, the tea boy, and a low-skilled secretary all counted. At the time, it was nearly impossible to attract any Saudis for these jobs, and it is still hard today. We practically had to beg Saudis to work for us, so we could complete our Saudization quota. As we grew larger, we were able to attract Saudis for higher positions with high salaries. But for startup ventures, who generally cannot afford to do this, the best bet is to bring in more partners or develop an attractive incentive system. Even so, in most cases, young graduates are focused on establishing a career and are rarely interested in taking such a risk. The only way to get through the dilemma of getting work permits is discussed in Tip 64. It is an interesting challenge all companies should look into before launching their startup in the MENA region.

 RELATED TIPS: 60, 61

How do you like the MVP for the new car?

Releasing the "minimum viable product" quickly in a lean startup helps jump-start a new venture. Any venture.

Adjusting your product after starting operations, a.k.a. "pivoting," is the cornerstone of the lean startup methodology. "Lean startup" is a method for developing businesses and products first proposed in 2011 by Eric Ries. It encourages the launch of a "minimal viable product" (MVP) which is then tweaked and improved based on customer feedback.[34]

The explosion in the number of Internet users and increases in the functionality of cloud computing and shared resources have driven the cost of launching a product down. Instead of spending countless days in the expensive perfection of the product prior to launch, then taking customer feedback, and ultimately releasing multiple versions, you can start by producing a working prototype and testing it on customers. Positive customer feedback is a cornerstone of a successful product. Your team has to be ready, with a flexible design that may change over and over until the product is perfected to your customers' satisfaction. Once you have a product that captures the essence of your idea, you can release it to a controlled group of your customers and test it for feedback. If you make your design flexible enough, you can adjust your product quickly in reaction to customer input, eventually reaching the best combination as you go. This lean startup is a structured method for pivoting your business while simultaneously designing the product and collecting customer feedback on it.

---

[34] Ries, Eric. *The Lean Startup: How Today's Entrepreneurs Use Continuous Innovation to Create Radically Successful Businesses.* (New York: Crown Publishing, 2011), p. 11.

Working with a minimal viable product is a very effective method for reducing costs until the product is perfect while proving the concept to investors at the same time. A very interesting example I came across is from Lit Motors. "Danny Kim of Lit Motors invented an appealing little vehicle that has, as he says, "The romance and efficiency of a motorcycle with the safety and efficiency of a car." It essentially cuts the car in half, leaving just the part the driver sits in (plus a really cool set of wheels). The idea is for something sustainable and affordable—"the same thing the Model-T did," as he puts it.

Jumping into mass production of something as complex as an automobile is incredibly difficult, so he started by testing out a showroom before he built the cars. When he found that nearly 16% of people who walked into this simulated showroom were ready to put down money on the spot, he had demonstrated enough marketability to start hand-building the vehicles for individual sale. He sold out of machines before even getting Series A funding."[35] This example shows that the lean startup methodology can be applied to almost any sector, not just the tech sector. The concept is a common-sense one: don't spend the cash until you're sure. Try to test as thoroughly as possible, with the least cost and the least effort. Having said that, building an MVP requires a lot of hard work; you need to release your MVP without turning off your customers, and you

[35]Regan, Lisa and Sarah Milstein. "Lean Startup Beyond the Tech Sector." Startup Lesson Learned blog. July 25, 2013. http://www.startuplessonslearned.com/2013/07/lean-startup-beyond-tech-sector.html.

need to get them excited, while giving them only a taste of the features they should get from the "real" product.

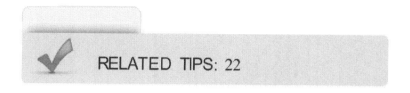

RELATED TIPS: 22

A retail startup needs an exclusive catchment area[36] in its zone more than it needs an IP.

---

[36] Catchment area: The area from which a business's customers are drawn.

I have mentioned in related tips the problems that are associated with copycats and with having limited protection for your ideas and trademarks. Further problems may arise if your business depends on an outlet location and the attraction of exclusive traffic. Zoning[37] is not enforced in all parts of the world, and even if it is, catchment areas within the zone may not necessarily be allocated. In Saudi Arabia, there is catchment area enforcement for schools, mosques, and gas stations. Some municipalities abide by this enforcement, and some don't.

When a catchment area is enforced for a particular business, it protects against a competitor opening up shop within a particular distance from that business's outlet. If the first shop has gained popularity in an area, then it's only fair to let that shop's owners enjoy it, and not allow others to come in and reap the benefits from the first store's investment in educating customers in that area. Imagine a scenario in which a burger joint opens up in an area, promotes itself to customers, and gradually gains a regular, local clientele. Soon afterward, another burger joint opens up next to the first one, or in its area, making the same offers. This situation is unfair to the first burger joint, which will have incurred operational losses before customers become aware of the business and start frequenting it. A catchment area protects a business's investment from being undermined in this way.

---

[37] Zoning: Predefined land use within the city determined by the municipality.

Saudi Arabia is full of classic examples of the chaos that results from unregulated zones. In the '70s, a small joint imported some special fried chicken machines and opened up under the name Broasted Chicken. Suddenly, whole streets were filled with joints carrying the word "Broast." The broast wars ended a few years later with one giant triumphant: Al Baik, mentioned in the example for Tip 9. Similar examples can be found in every type of retail or supply store. Therefore, it is essential for an entrepreneur starting a business in Saudi to check whether it is possible to get zone protection for the new outlet. Otherwise, opportunists who don't want to take a risk, can't do market research, or lack originality will wait in the bushes for someone else to make a successful outlet, and then simply copy that person's idea. And having an opportunist open up next to you is not the only worry. As described in related tips, in an unregulated zone, it is even possible for others to copy your name with or without variation. That can be a double disaster for a startup store. Your only protection from this sort of opportunism is to develop a point of difference to ensure that no one can acquire your customers. If you don't feel you can provide a point of difference to protect yourself, make sure to consider this risk, and be prepared to deal with it.

RELATED TIPS: 16, 38, 40, 67

Try to think outside the box.

Getting to your customers is not easy. B2B and B2C have their own unique challenges.

Nothing comes easy in life, and business is no different. If you are running a B2B business, then your relationships are your primary marketing tools, at least in the beginning. Saudi Arabia is a country governed by strong family and tribal connections. It is rare for someone to give a project to a company that he or one of his relatives does not know. The more the product costs, the less likely it is that a startup will get its first break selling to a stranger. For startups, making a break into the circle requires years. The first projects the startup lands are key to breaking into that circle. First projects are usually acquired through founder connections to the business circles.

Those that feel they cannot break into these circles, are less connected, or are looking to run a simple business, usually choose to go into the B2C market. However, the headache that comes with dealing with everyday consumers is not any less than that of dealing with conservative businesspeople. In addition to all the hard work required to gain customer trust, get first traction, and conduct extensive research into customer taste and acceptance of the goods or services, entrepreneurs also have to take extensive regulations into account.

It is a common practice for entrepreneurs trying to create a B2B startup to find a partner that can guarantee the first set of projects. The more expensive the product is, the more difficult it will be to penetrate the business circles in the country. As explained in Tip 59, every league has its players. Nobody really pays attention to Little League players, and their main problems usually arise with *municipal officers. Most small businesses close down due to insufficient market research prior to launch. There is little innovation in the SME sectors in Saudi Arabia, as most of this sector comprises retail and food outlets. However, students with a foreign education are coming back with fresh ideas, and many of them are turning to entrepreneurship. Some of those have started opening retail shops with different ideas, and with the objective of creating potentially international brands. This can be seen in the recent proliferation of new chocolate, coffee, and clothing retailers, in addition to the food trucks licensed lately. Other tech graduates are creating apps to cover local, regional, and international needs. Launching an app involves fewer regulations and less red tape than launching a retail business. It is important to keep in mind, however, that an app that breaks any of the country's taboos will be taken off-line and the founder fined. Recent laws covering electronic media have increased fines to up to $150K and ten years in jail. Most of the apps cited as examples in this book were launched by students returning from Europe, North America, and Australia. Releasing an app may require less regulatory requirements, particularly if the operation was fully online, yet, that app has to adhere to government rules. Any app or online platform that breaks such rules will be shut down and the owners will be fined. The maximum sentence for electronic crimes is a fine of $150K and a jail sentence of up to ten years.*

 RELATED TIPS: 15, 59

We love the idea of the "all-female makeup delivery service," but we don't have a budget for drivers to take you around.

It's still tough for a woman in Saudi Arabia to make it in business due to regulatory hindrances. Make sure you address cultural risks when starting your business.

Saudi Arabia has a very strict society, if not one of the strictest. However, with the reforms HRH Prince Mohammed Bin Salman has initiated, a lot has changed positively, especially for women. It was only a few years back that women were first allowed to handle their own transactions in government offices. Before, a businesswoman had to have a male advocate, and many times these men turned out to be opportunists who took advantage of their female associates. To really put this in perspective, consider that the first lawyer's license was handed out to a woman in October 2013.

Today, many of the previous restrictions have been lifted, and women are more strongly present in the workplace. The Ministry of Labor has introduced many regulations to encourage the presence of women in the workforce. In fact, one of the main objectives of Vision 2030 is to increase women's presence in the workforce.[38] One of the major restrictions was lifted with the historical decision allowing women to drive in June 2018.

However, restrictions remain, and a woman founding or co-founding a business must take into consideration local laws and regulations, which are changing almost monthly. It is very important to assess the situation from all angles if you intend to hire female employees, or if you are a woman who would like to start a business in Saudi. Even now, the entry of foreign female staff members of companies doing business in Saudi Arabia carries some restrictions, particularly in age. Obtaining a business visit visa for a woman is more

[38] NTP 2.0 overview July 18, 2017.

complex than obtaining one for a man. Once in the country, women have to be dressed up and fully covered with an *abaya*[39] at all times. In the service sector, many jobs still cannot be occupied by women, including waiter, driver, bellboy, valet, and others. The mixing of women and men in the workplace is generally prohibited, except on a very limited basis. The general rule is that the sexes should be isolated from one another, although minor mixing is allowed by work nature. If a function requires continuous mixing, then it will probably not be allowed. This does not include jobs in the medical sector, which have been deemed a "necessity" for a long time. A woman starting a business in Saudi Arabia is well advised to think of the hindrances she will face, from not being allowed in some government buildings, to not being permitted to create a startup in certain professions.

I met Afrah Albliwi, an aspiring female entrepreneur who has launched her own business specialized in wedding photography. And even though this activity sounds like a purely female activity given that Saudi weddings are segregated and such a business line should be supported, Afrah's experience was different. A few years after her graduation from college, in 2010, she broke her way through this field at twenty-six years of age and without experience. But because of her gender, she faced great difficulties, unfortunately. Among these difficulties, was the fact that it took two years to get her license from the Ministry of Information. During these two years, she could not work, and she had to pay rent for her location. Renting a location is a prerequisite for obtaining a

---

[39] Abaya: Traditional black cloak covering the whole body.

municipal license, which in turn is a prerequisite for getting a Ministry of Labor and GOSI license as explained in Tip 23 and Appendix 3. Add to that the municipality required the location to be on a major street, which meant more expensive rent too. She could not do any work inside her fully equipped location either, so she had to work from her home. She had to install printing equipment there too.

When she finally got her license, she could not obtain a visa for assistants, nor could she convince locals to take on such a hard labor job. The job involves carrying heavy equipment and setting up locations. These obstacles were technicalities related to her CR being a female one. Legacy labor laws allowed obtaining foreign work permits for few activities such as tailoring and apparel sales. These laws were not updated with the required speed to cope with growing development in the entrepreneurial scene in Saudi Arabia, particularly when it comes to women. Note that such hindrances would not exist if the business entity were a company and not a private enterprise as Afrah's. So Would Afrah need to partner with someone just to bypass these laws?[40]

However, regardless of all of the above, Afrah prevailed. No obstacles can stop the perseverance and strong willpower of the entrepreneur. Afrah could not work in KSA, so she moved her shop to Dubai, which should not be a surprise knowing that she obtained her license in just forty-eight hours! Now she works in different activities including electronic marketing and importing printing equipment for advertising, in addition to her original

---

[40] A recent update to corporate laws allowed the creation of a single-partner company.

photography. Needless to say, Afrah's sales grew from twenty events per year to one hundred, and doubled after that. She aims now to grow by 500%. Who's to dare this entrepreneur?

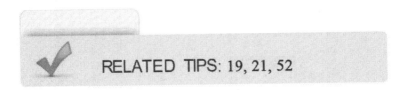

RELATED TIPS: 19, 21, 52

An ability to manage cash flow is a necessary qualification for running your startup. If you are not good with numbers, learn how to work with them.

In his book *Entrepreneurial Finance*, Dr. Steven Rogers asserts that entrepreneurs who are not good with numbers will never achieve high growth in their startups.[41] Managing cash flow means monitoring the cash in and controlling the cash out so that you have enough money to cover your operational expenses. This is a daily challenge every small business owner faces. If you can't do it, don't start a business.

Handling of routine expenditures is one of the things you can't outsource: you, or one of your co-founders, has to be in touch with the daily operations to make decisions on who to pay, to push collections, and to get deals from suppliers, banks, and customers to make sure the company never runs out of cash. You cannot hire an accountant to do that for you. Even if you do, you have to be able to make decisions with them, and not follow them blindly, or they may rip you off. Dr. Rogers gives a couple of great examples of just that scenario. (Check the reference above.)

In 2007, as the CEO of Alcantara Group, I signed a contract with the Saudi Ministry of Defense for one of the largest deals for EMR (electronic medical records) in the history of the country. It included installing the German Nexus system in all Defense Hospitals, which numbered around twenty-six, in addition to over sixty clinics. So far, so good, right? Well, the government only pays on receipt, works on fixed contracts, allows no payment for mods, and provides no down payments. This was very different from

---

[41] Rogers, Steven. *Entrepreneurial Finance*, Second Edition, (New York: McGraw Hill, 2007), Chapter 5.

the normal terms we had agreed to with our German supplier Nexus AG, our Swedish supplier IFS AB, and our American suppliers Sun Microsystems and Oracle (which later became one company). All of those contracts needed to be paid in ninety days or so. This imbalance meant that I would have to finance the gap between the customer payments and the supplier payments. The balancing act I had to play was to bridge the difference between my customer and my suppliers, so my company wouldn't get squeezed in the middle. For the largest supplier, Nexus, I had to fly to Germany and convince them to honor the government terms and only expect to be paid when we did. The Swedes, with whom I had a longer-standing relationship, were already familiar with our environment. Sun had to be satisfied with letters of credit, which could only be done through a bank agreement. It took our bank six months to approve our line of credit, and it almost killed me trying to keep everyone on board. The customer was demanding delivery of the hardware, and the suppliers were demanding money. The project could not start without hardware in place. While waiting for the hardware to arrive, we finally managed to kick off minor consulting work, after convincing the customer's project manager to understand our point of view. This balancing act I performed felt like the ones you see in the circus. Many times, we entrepreneurs feel we are in a circus, juggling all the balls and trying to please all the audiences.

RELATED TIPS: 53

...Therefore, if you invest in my startup, you will get returns of 500%.

A presentation is like a stage play. Just like an actor, you need to rehearse, engage, and carefully pick your punch lines.

As an entrepreneur, one of the primary skills you have to master is presenting. Whether you are a B2B or a B2C business, you need to communicate with customers, investors, your employees, and your board. You may be able to get away with a bad presentation to the office geeks, who either don't know how to present either or can't tell you that you suck. Outsiders may keep quiet, but will never give you what you came for, and that is not the outcome you would like to have.

When you are preparing for a presentation, think of yourself as an actor in a leading role. You should consider your delivery, your message, and your objective. You should be well dressed, showered, and looking and smelling great. Part of your delivery may be in the form of PowerPoint and videos; these should be short, visual, and to the point. You should pick your words carefully after studying your customer and the message you would like to bring across. Studying your customer is like studying your audience in a stage play. Content that is not suitable for children should not go into a children's play. Content that is funny in the US may be offensive in other regions of the world. A long, boring presentation can throw off your audience. The information you present should be enough to get the audience excited without scaring them away. There are tons of articles on the subject, so Google some of them. It is advisable to rehearse many times until you get it right. Do a dry run in front of people you trust who will give you honest advice.

My Alcantara team was presenting our software solution to a customer back in 2008. They wanted a simple financial solution for their lucrative but operationally small company. The customer had a fear of complex systems and they had heard about failed ERP (enterprise resource planning) implementations. We rehearsed the presentation internally with our team many times. I kept telling them to keep it short and simple. I went with them through every single slide and cut out tons of unnecessary information. The goal was to show that we fit their requirement of a simple system to implement and operate, and not to show our muscle. Had they been looking at Oracle or SAP, which we used to compete with most of the time, that would have been the strategy, but they weren't. I went through the live demo, and we tailored a nice, simple walk-through of basic features with sample data taken from the client. On the big day, everything was going smoothly and the consultant stuck to the scenario. Even so, I had to intervene more than once to reaffirm the simplicity message. Then, just as we were about to close the sale, the consultant decided to flex his muscle by going into extra features. His system hung, and his unrehearsed extra demo failed. The customer suddenly got the fear that the system was very complex and would not be usable by his staff. (I should add that the consultant choking on his tea and barfing in front of the customer did not help either.)

We had gone outside of the rehearsed scenario, and it shook the customer's confidence in our entire offering. Sometimes, saying too much is as bad as saying too little.

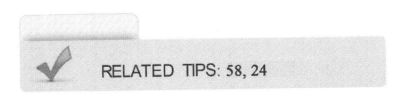

RELATED TIPS: 58, 24

34

Launching a product does not equate to launching a startup. You need to spend more money and exert much more effort to do the latter.

As I will explain in Tip 41, launching a product has become much easier and much cheaper due to advances in technology, high Internet penetration, the cloud, and shared services. But launching a product does not equate to launching a company.

You may be able to launch one app out of your bedroom, but as this app becomes popular and needs to be upgraded, you will need to talk to customers and solve their problems. You will also need staff to carry out those functions, and once you start needing that, then you need a business. Requiring staff is not the only reason to have a business; finances, taxation, marketing, and delivery are many other reasons you simply can't run a real business from your bedroom or garage. The process of building a business has not changed much even with all the advances in the cyber world, and it still requires almost the same amount of time and effort.

I work closely with Badir Incubators. An incubator by nature does not provide funding, though it saves a startup a lot of money in terms of basic facility, utility, and support services. Many app developers are happy that they are able to launch their app from the incubator and eventually graduate. Eventually, as their business expands, they realize that it's time for them to leave their "parents' house" and do it on their own. Unfortunately, those with no post-launch strategy face a grim reality when they have to pay their own bills. They suddenly need office space, a social media team, and a delivery and support organization. They need to stay close to their customers to provide upgrades. Those who don't have a plan usually fail to survive. Unfortunately, many of the incubator program's tenants die due to lack of funding. Unless the incubator has close ties with investors or hosts an accelerator-like demo day, "incubatees" have to find investors on their own, and most of the time they fail to do it. This is why many incubators either are owned by or tightly linked with some kind of fund. If you have to pick between a number of incubators and an accelerator, consider the one with better financing options. This gives you the comfort of having someone to give you a chance. Trying to find an investor on your own can be a very hard task.

RELATED TIPS: 24,58

Being your own boss is tempting. But remember that in your startup you will be doing a number of jobs, where you do all the paying.

As I stated in related tips, being your own boss is an illusion: as the owner of a startup, you will have multiple bosses. In addition, you will not feel like a boss, because you may have no one else to delegate to. So what's the use of being a boss when you have five jobs all covered by yourself?

The glamour of being your own boss gives an illusion of freedom, less work, and more free time. But working five or more jobs in your startup is not fun; it's a lot of work. And if you are serious and don't have a second source of income—or any source of income—it can put tremendous pressure on you to produce results. Sure, the business card reading "CEO," or "managing director," or any other title you choose to give yourself is gratifying, but the reality is that you are going to work very hard to earn that title.

When I first started out in my consulting business, BASE Consulting, back in 1994, I only had one part-time assistant, because I could not afford to have one full time. I had to be my own accountant, with the help of some minor accounting software called MYOB (mind your own business), tea boy, janitor, administrator, lawyer, technician, driver, and of course managing director. That was a fake title because I managed no one but myself. At the end, I realized being my own boss was just an illusion.

You will always have a boss—you just report to them differently. When you are a junior employee in a company, you may report as frequently as every day. The more you go up the ladder, the more responsibility you have and the less frequently you have to report. However, with time, the stakes become higher and you become more responsible. The fear of having to pay a price for a mistake will always be there.

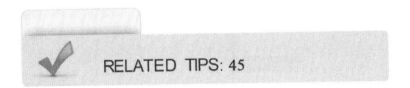

RELATED TIPS: 45

I have been enjoying growth for the last 40 years, and I want to branch out, but I'm not sure how to be in two places at the same time.

Every startup is an SME but not every SME is a startup. If your business model does not scale to high multiples in 2–5 years, then you are not a startup.

One very important attribute of every startup is that it usually has few people in it, probably founders only, and produces limited turnover. This makes it an SME (small-to-medium enterprise). But startups are more glamorous than SMEs, not just because of the name, but because startups usually create more value than an SME.

The main defining feature of a startup is its high-growth, high-value, high-scalability nature. This is why most startups are usually found in narrow high-growth technology fields such as ICT (information and communication technology) and biotechnology. But what really determines that your venture is a startup is its scalability. If you cannot scale your business in a short period, then you should revise your business model. If you feel that the business you chose cannot scale and provide high multiples of growth for you and your investors, then you are certainly not a startup.

Scalability and fast growth are attributes of a startup, and a qualification for venture capital funding. This is why many lists celebrating startups focus on their fast growth—a sign of their scalability. The very first award my company Alcantara won was the Saudi Fast Growth 100 (SFG 100). It was the first competition of its kind in Saudi Arabia. The Saudi Arabia General Investment Authority (SAGIA) brought in a team from Harvard to evaluate and induct Saudi startups to the list. Allworld describes themselves on their own website[42] as follows: "In 1998 the three AllWorld Founders (Anne Habiby, Deirdre Coyle, and Harvard Business School Professor Michael Porter)

---

[42] http://www.allworldlive.com/about/overview

helped create the US Inner City 100 with Inc. magazine. We set out to find and rank fast-growing private companies in America's poor urban communities. We were amazed to see how swiftly the market organized around the Inner City 100 information. From no funds, soon there were many investing in inner-city companies, and President Clinton changed national banking policy based on our data. At the Inner City 100 tenth anniversary, eight thousand companies applied and were nominated, and we set our sights worldwide creating AllWorld Network."

IFS Arabia had grown by 500% between 1997 and 2002, with little recognition. However, when we grew as Alcantara group—which included IFS Arabia—by another 431% between 2003 and 2007, we won tenth place on the SFG 100 in 2009. We went on to win the award in 2010 and 2011. These awards focus on growth because they want to encourage startups to scale. We won the award during the most successful years of our business.

 RELATED TIPS: 15, 59

Your unregistered brand, slogan, or trademark can be stolen as easily as taking a screenshot from your website.

Copycats may just enjoy your free brand recognition and not necessarily copy your business model or secret recipe. The burden of proving that you are the original owner of the brand is on you, and it will take you years to do it in court, while the thief enjoys free branding. If you reach your expansion stage, having your brand copied is a higher risk, compared to the risk for an unknown company, which can easily switch to a new logo. A company at a later stage may be forced to take the long and expensive road of a lawsuit.

In countries where trademark protection is not strongly enforced, or where lawsuits are lengthy and expensive, brand theft can pose a major risk. Even in countries where trademark protection is enforced, international thievery can be a big problem. It can be extremely difficult to sue a copycat in China when you live in Jordan, for example, even if you have registered your trademark in China. If you are an SME this can be just as challenging, and as threatening. Registering your trademark is something you should do prior to expanding your business. You should also make sure that the registration jurisdiction covers the areas you want to expand into and protects your trademark.

In Saudi Arabia, the easiest thing to do is to use someone else's logo or trademark. So far, there is no link between trademark offices, which are in the Ministry of Commerce, and Municipality offices, which license signs. If you are a non-retail business and would like to use a logo on your letterhead, all you have to do is print the logo and the name on your stationery and register under your company name at the local Chamber of Commerce. They only verify that your legal name and CR number are printed on the stationery. Many businesses do that in fine print while putting any logo and commercial name on top. Registering the actual trademark takes place in another department. Some take advantage of this discrepancy and simply copy logos, which can ease the process of starting a business. If you are starting a small business, say a burger joint, you can easily call it Burger King! If your conscience doesn't bother you, you may alter the logo a little while waiting for the real Burger King to sue you. If they do, there is no fine—you will simply be asked to change your logo. I myself was a victim of online theft. The name BASE Consulting was created by me for my first startup. It's an acronym for "Business Automation and Systems Engineering." A few months after I created my website, the full name with the acronym was stolen by a company in the USA. I know that because I was searching for my site and found theirs. There is another company in Toronto with the same name but without the acronym, which is older than mine. In this case, I did not copy their name, and they did not copy my acronym; the overlap was a pure coincidence.

A recent example of the same problem involves two brothers in Jeddah who ran a doughnut shop. When they split, one of them got the business; however, the other brother, who was bought out, opened a new chain and simply used the same logo. After a few years in court, he was asked to change his logo and sign. Taking advantage of the loose trademark protection laws, using the same colors and fonts and a slight variation of the logo, he used *the same name, but in the plural instead!!! His brother could not sue this time.*

RELATED TIPS: 16, 29, 38, 40, 67

...And we expect our share price to soar, as we intend to pirate more apps this year.

IP is not the only way to protect your idea. Small startups rarely can afford IP enforcement. Consider other means.

Many startups get locked on the notion of protecting their idea by means of Intellectual Property protection, or IP. Applying for IP protection involves an expensive and lengthy process of filing, registering, paying fees, and monitoring copycats. In some countries, including Saudi Arabia and many Middle Eastern, African, and Asian countries, IP protection cannot be effectively enforced. Even in countries where it is possible to enforce it, an average lawsuit can cost up to $5 million. Many large corporations have found it easier to buy their competitors than to sue them, which has opened a new market, further encouraging copycats. Neither of these solutions—a lawsuit or a buyout—is feasible for most startups. So what's the solution?

IP is only one way of protecting your idea or venture. Perfecting a POD (point of difference) can help your business gain market leadership and earn an early competitive advantage. Building a business model around your unique POD can help you gain a lead that makes it difficult for your competitors to catch you. Instead of wasting your time and money protecting your idea via IP registration, you should utilize that time and money in more effective efforts that may lead to far better results.

Three German brothers have founded an incubator that mainly harbors copycats. They have made millions off this practice. "Alexander, Marc, and Oliver Samwer are the three brothers behind the infamous incubator Rocket Internet. They first found success by investing in startups like StudiVZ, also known as the German Facebook. They are also the minds behind German auction site Alando, *sold to eBay in 1999 for $54 million, and mobile content platform Jamba!, which sold to Verizon in 2004 for $273 million."* [43] *Rocket Internet provides just one example of how difficult it is to protect yourself from copycats, even if you have IP protection. Facebook failed in suing StudiVZ. Many others failed to enforce their IP also. Apple lost the GUI war in the 1990s to Microsoft and is chasing Samsung on iPad and iPhone IP infringements in the new millennium. All these big-name examples should drive home the point that spending money protecting your startup via expensive IP registration may not work. You can protect yourself and your idea better by thinking of the POD and creating competitive advantage and enough customers to make potential copycats think twice before stealing your original ideas. Or you can simply become a copycat yourself. If you can't beat them, join them! (See tip 40.)*

 RELATED TIPS: 16, 29, 37, 40, 67

[43] McHugh, Molly. "Attack of the Startup Clones: How Copycat Companies Are Changing the Tech Industry." Digital Trends Blog. April 14, 2012.
http://www.digitaltrends.com/features/attack-of-the-startup-clones-how-copycat-companies-are-changing-the-tech-industry/.

Chapter 3

The Launch Stage

At this stage, startups refine their business model and improve the efficiency of their customer acquisition process. This stage comes after you have validated the business model with your first set of customers. Startups at this stage should be able to efficiently acquire customers and sustain their operations at least partly from returns.

Key Activities: Refining value proposition, improving user experience based on feedback from the first set of customers, optimizing conversion of prospects to customers, achieving viral growth, developing a means to scale the business and improve customer acquisition.

Funding Type: Angels and micro-VCs.

Okay, guys, we spent all our seed money on branding and advertising. Now we need to raise money to create the actual product.

Some of the best companies have smaller marketing budgets, as their own consumers are now advocates in social media networks.

Corporate identity designs, logos, and matters related to traditional marketing tools are important. Once you have nailed them in the beginning of your venture and settled on your strategy and promise as stated in related tips, your focus should be turned more to delivery and less to hype. The core of marketing is for your customer to be *delighted*, not satisfied, and your marketing efforts must be focused on ensuring that and assessing it on a regular basis. This does not mean that you should not do marketing and branding. Just don't waste your limited cash on fancy designs that cost hundreds and thousands of dollars. Even some of the most famous logos in the world cost very little. Nike's logo cost only $35, and it is one of the most recognized in the world.[44]

Philip Kotler, the father of marketing, asserts in his book: "Because social media is low cost and bias-free, it will be the future for marketing communication. Connections between friends on social networking sites such as Facebook and MySpace can also help companies base their insights into the market."[45] In today's world, connecting with customers is very important. The good news is that social media costs very little, and you have unlimited space to communicate all that you want about your product or service to consumers. In the old days, you had to pay for expensive airtime, and therefore your logos and ads had to be well designed for such expensive media. Nowadays, with social marketing, everything has become cheaper.

---

[44] Hughes, Mark, "Logos that Became Legends: Icons from the World of Advertising." *The Independent*. August 6, 2012.

[45] Kotler, Philip et al. *From Products to Consumers to the Human Spirit: Marketing 3.0.* (Hoboken, New Jersey: John Wiley & Sons, 2010), p. 9.

The social media boom has changed the way customer engagement takes place. Before this shift in popular media consumption, you got to your customers primarily via advertising. Direct marketing served only a limited type of business, which was mainly B2B. As a result, perfecting your logos and marketing material was key. The only way a startup could dream of engaging millions is via mass-market advertising. Times have changed. Customers are not so interested in company ads anymore, but in real stories and recommendations by other customers. They get that via social media platforms such as Facebook, Twitter, Instagram, and YouTube.

My wife used to run the marketing department for a group of clinics called SABA Medical. She started using social media marketing back in 2012. There has been a great shift from the use of traditional marketing tools to social ones. As a result of continuous measurement of customer acquisition rates, more money has been shifted to social media. One example is a $100K billboard situated in one of the major streets of Jeddah, which traditionally brought in 13% of new customers to SABA Medical per year. Social media drew the same percentage with one-tenth of the cost when the company started using it in 2012. In 2013, 25% of the new patients came from social media. The billboard was taken down, as social media was more efficient for acquiring customers. Today, the quarter of the clinic's patients that are drawn from social media are acquired at a rate of $1.50 per new patient, *compared to $20 per new patient using traditional advertising a few years back.*

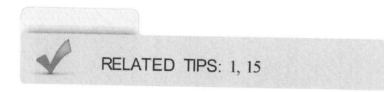

RELATED TIPS: 1, 15

If you can't beat the copycats, join them.

This may sound unethical, but as demonstrated in the example in Tip 38, many businesses have flourished in Europe and Asia under this business model. In fact, a reputable incubator has the growth of copycats as its de facto mission. Rocket Internet is not alone. Companies like Russian-based Fast Lane Ventures have also indulged in the copycat business. Fast Lane Ventures is home to PinMe and a Zappos clone it sold to another, larger, Zappos clone.[46]

Adapting the business model of a successful app from another country to your region has an advantage of allowing you to jump or shorten the ideation phase and parts of the validation phase. All you have to worry about is the applicability of the idea in your region. That can be verified by a simple market assessment and control group testing. On the downside, if the original owner decides to launch a localized version for your region, they may become serious competition, or could simply wipe you off the face of the cloud!

I was invited to the venture lab competition at KAUST in May 2012 as a judge. The contestants were the first graduates of the school, which is geared toward economic development and encourages entrepreneurship. A few of the contestants had actually copied their models from international apps. One of them proposed a unique compression technique as a POD, which they filed a patent for. All of them failed to position themselves among

---

[46] McHugh, Molly. "Attack of the Startup Clones: How Copycat Companies Are Changing the Tech Industry." Digital Trends Blog. April 14, 2012. http://www.digitaltrends.com/features/attack-of-the-startup-clones-how-copycat-companies-are-changing-the-tech-industry/.

competitors, however, and didn't state their competitive advantage. KAUST later refined the way their students presented to make sure they wouldn't qualify if they didn't follow the right process. However, the point is, if you want to copy, make sure you do a good job, or at least make sure you add features suitable for your region that give you some kind of an edge. Sometimes the local environment is not ready for such an app. One of the KAUST contestants had a discount coupon notification app. It depended upon identifying the stores which had discounts most suitable for the user nearby, based on his or her current location. This has been successful and implemented by some other international apps such as Coupon Sherpa and Yowza. However, most of the relevant retailers in this app's region were not on Google Maps yet and were generally not tech savvy. Additionally, online shopping was not as popular in Saudi Arabia back then, nor is sending gifts by mail on occasions a regional habit, unlike in Western Europe or the USA. All these factors contributed to the problems the app had with traction, which eventually led to its failure. When localizing a successful business, make sure you consider the local behavior and business environment to ensure success.

 RELATED TIPS: 16, 18, 38

I'm the best midwife in town, and I'm ready for delivery.

The low cost of application rollouts has made it easier to launch products.

Before the bursting of the dot-com bubble in 2001, Internet users were fewer, in the millions, while now it's a few billion. Application writers at the time required much more money to launch their apps, took more time to get feedback, and had to release version after version. Marketing, packaging, cutting CDs, and shipping all cost a considerable amount of money.

Cloud computing, app stores, and the spread of the Internet have changed the way apps are released. You can use Amazon Web Services (AWS) or similar services to host your app for a few tens of dollars, launch your app from your own home, create a marketing campaign via social media for very small amounts, and potentially reach over a billion users in cyberspace. This is a chance your peers did not have a few years ago, and it should be taken advantage of.

When I moved back from the USA to Saudi Arabia in the late '90s, my first idea was to start a software company and sell software to worldwide users. One of the products that did not exist at the time was a "word processor" with Arabic support. When I started doing my feasibility study for the project, I realized that once the software was created we would need to cut CDs, design jewel boxes, and find a local manufacturer. At the time, the cost of recording CDs was high, and we could not do it in-house. Another problem was printing manuals, which carried a very high cost as well. After all that, we would need to design a package, put everything together, and ship to users. Marketing the product using advertising, flyers, and brochures would rack up design, printing, and distribution fees. Once the product was out, we would need a tech support team to answer the phone and send emails, as web and social media communication were not there yet. By comparison, if you wanted to launch an app today, you could do so with a single click from your bedroom. Think how much easier it has become, and take advantage of that. I could not afford to launch my word processor project at the time, and Microsoft made an Arabic version of MS Word a few years later.

RELATED TIPS: 34

Diaspora networks are a good resource for startups. Your network of relatives or your ethnic group may serve as a good resource for launching your startup.

The use of diaspora[47] networks has been going on for a long time. Many ethnic groups have been known to be successful in the various countries of their migration. Some neighborhoods have become branded for their famous ethnic groups, like the "Chinatowns" in many Western cities.

A new immigrant entrepreneur comes to a new city or country with no network, lacking knowledge about the ins and outs of the market, and sometimes even lacking funding. Diaspora networks often serve as virtual incubators to such people. In the Arab world, tribal or similar village connections have served similar purposes for a long time.

Hadhramis (Southern Yemeni) and Palestinians are very good examples of people who have created strong, successful ethnic communities in Saudi Arabia and all over the world. Indians and Chinese are particularly successful in working together within their diaspora networks worldwide. Shahid Abbasi is a Pakistani-Canadian engineer that worked for me in my first two startups. When on board, he helped me acquire talent, and his contacts were always from Pakistan. He lived in the Pakistani diaspora neighborhood north of Jeddah, Saudi Arabia, at the time, before moving to Texas and creating a very successful startup, which he later merged with BullseyeEvaluation in 2006. I met with him again back in 2010 when he visited me in my office in Jeddah. I asked him then how he had managed to

---

[47] Word of Greek origin meaning "a scattered population with a common origin in a smaller geographic area."

penetrate the market and make it in Texas in just a few years. His answer was that he had relatives that had helped him start, fund, and get his first set of customers. He is not alone. Many Middle Eastern entrepreneurs get help from their fellow countrymen when in the US, Europe, or other Middle Eastern countries. Almost all of the food carts in central New York are run by Egyptians nowadays. In Saudi Arabia, this ethnic selectivity has developed to the extent that certain professions have become monopolized by other nationalities. Tire change and lubes by Yemenis, gourmet restaurants and advertising by Lebanese, bakeries by Syrians, and grocery stores by Bengalis, just to name a few.

If I could fit one on your head, your "Ghutra" would not fly with the wind.

Sometimes your market is not ready for cutting-edge technology, and sometimes technology may not be ready for your ambitions.

In related tips, I mentioned that markets in some countries are not ready for cutting-edge technology even if it's already a hit in advanced and industrial nations. But there are cases when the problem requires a solution that does not exist. Some businesspeople are interested in taking risks with something new, as long as it does not affect their mainstream business. These are not the majority, but they do exist.

Steve Jobs's edge was in "spotting a market filled with second-rate products" and then shopping for technology to make a first-rate product. For example, it took him six months to find a suitable hard drive at Toshiba that was small enough for the iPod prototype, and even then it would not be ready for another four months. Jobs signed an exclusive deal with Toshiba to develop the new hard drive for Apple, and then signed up a talented engineer to lead the design team. This is how the iPod was born.[48] Earlier, he had a vision for a way to make music downloads easier for everyone, so he bought a product that allowed users to make playlists and burn music, molded that product to fit his vision, and named it iTunes. Twenty years before that, he wanted computers to be used by everyone, so he jumped onto Xerox's star. His visions led the technology and not the other way around.

Back in 1999, tablets were not on the market yet, but they were common in research labs, where they were called "pen-based computers." They were a big research topic, and I was lucky to be exposed to them through my supervisor Wayne Citrin at CU Boulder.[49] I thought of these products

[48] Isaacson, Walter. *Steve Jobs.* (New York: Simon & Schuster, 2011), Chapter 30.
[49] Takayuki, Dan et al. "Potentials and Limitations of Pen-Based Computers." *Proceedings of the ACM Conference on Computer Science*, 1993, p. 536-539.

when a nephew of the group chairman, one of Saudi Arabia's top billionaires, came to me and said: "I have a problem I would like you to solve." The problem was that the chairman always had to be followed by tons of papers to sign on airplanes, as he was constantly traveling, like most people of with his level of wealth, and his staff constantly needed his signatures and approvals on sensitive documents.

Electronic signing was in its infancy, and Saudi Arabia did not have the Internet yet. I designed a simple solution that resembled what iCloud does. I created a centralized repository for documents connected via a company Intranet to different offices, and to a tablet that the billionaire carried around. I was given an appointment to meet him in his mansion in April 1999. I ordered one of the few commercial tablets available from Siemens, but when checking the details of the device I had ordered, I found out that it did not have enough memory to run the applications required for the solution. I had to order more memory. My deadline was approaching, and there was no time to receive the memory and the device and install them locally. I would have looked really bad if the time for the meeting came and I did not have a device to demonstrate the solution! To fix this problem, I had to play a trick and have the device delivered to a friend in Boulder, who installed the extra memory and sent the device to me ready for the demo.

The prospect client loved the demo and advised me to work with his CEO to develop a final proposal. This would have been a deal of a lifetime for me at the time. Which encouraged me to demo the same idea to General Asad Alfraih, head of national security at the time. General Alfraih was a pioneer in automating Ministry of Interior functions. The idea was to have each field officer carry a tablet and report incidents remotely.

However, the cost of setting up the data center turned out to be too high to be functional. Linking all of his offices with expensive satellite Internet did not make sense to the CEO. The technology was not ready for the idea, and it was not feasible, so ultimately our prospect client decided to keep carrying paper and hiring extra labor rather than spending a few million dollars. I would assume he carries a tablet and saves documents on the cloud today, at a fraction of what it would have cost him thirteen years ago. It's interesting to note that Bill Gates released what he called a "tablet PC" in Comdex, Las Vegas, in November of that very same year. I was there and attended his keynote presentation. However, it took the technology and the consumers another ten years to accept the tablet or the iPad as a replacement for the PC. The delay was due to a lag in Internet penetration, costs, and the emergence of cloud computing. I should mention that Gen. Alfraih also approved the demo; however, the proposal never passed his own IT department, due to high costs too.

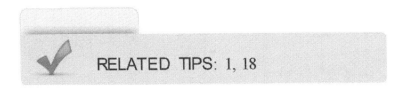

RELATED TIPS: 1, 18

Don't let media coverage fool you. You are not successful until your startup makes real cash and demonstrates profitability.

Many entrepreneurs get overwhelmed by the media coverage they receive after winning a seed fund or a business plan competition or getting a blog or an article to mention them. They get blinded to the extent that they think they have made it, when there is nothing further from the truth.

A startup is not successful until it starts making profits, or gains considerable traction with the potential of conversion into sales, and it is a long road to get there. You will need to perfect your business model, your product, your distribution, your costs, and so forth. Media coverage is cool if you can put it to your business's benefit or sales. But rarely will it seal your success on its own.

Back in 2012, a young aspiring entrepreneur won seed funding from one of the few seed fund programs available in Saudi Arabia. She used it to develop an application for patients with a certain terminal illness. She got coverage in the local media, and then she got some coverage from CNN and pan-Arabian TV stations. She got caught in the media bug and spent most of her time doing PR. When she tried to pitch for us at Sirb to get more angel funding, we were surprised at how much she focused on the coverage and how little on her traction and how she intended to grow her business. The information she presented about her expected returns was not focused and was not very convincing. She also failed to position her application among her competitors and identify her point of difference. A year after she launched her app, it still had not caught on and become a hit, and neither had it achieved minimum attractive traction. I think if she focused more on the business model, profitability, and selling, she could have achieved better results. She was not alone. Many founders catch the "media bug," get addicted to the spotlight, and forget their main mission, which is to sell and make profits. I'm not saying you should not do PR and marketing, but you should only do it if it builds up to you selling to your customers. That balance is something some startups fail to focus on.

Launching a startup is a tough job, probably tougher than any job you have had working for others.

One of the first incentives entrepreneurs think of when quitting their job to follow their dream is that they will have no boss. This means the freedom of showing up to work late and taking more holidays. Well, I have news for you: it will take you a very long time to get to that stage, if you ever do.

A boss is someone who holds enough power over you that you will actually listen to their instructions, either in fear of consequences or to gain their approval. Under that definition, you will have a number of bosses pushing you around for the first few years of your new venture. Your financiers will have many demands that you will jump and dance to meet. Your staff will create indirect pressure on you to be an example of performance, so you may as well forget about showing up late. On top of this, you will have to pay them at the end of every month, or they will leave you. Your first customers will probably have the most power over you, as you can't afford to lose them. Just think of what you will do to make them happy.

The early days of a startup require you to put in long hours and make sacrifices. Unless you are wealthy enough to pay your staff to work while you play, you have to be there as much as they are, if not more. If you don't show up early to work, your staff won't, or will not take you seriously. If you are one of the lucky ones that gets admitted into an accelerator, your accelerator becomes your boss. They will not offer you space, mentorship, and funding for free. They will interfere in your business very early on. They will dictate how it will scale and how it will appeal to your customers and co-investors. You can't show up late during this process, or fail to hit your milestones. Being your own boss brings more responsibilities, not fewer. If you are working on an app, the pressure of releasing it will make you work longer hours so you can launch it and start making money. Even if you are opening an outlet, you will work very hard to make sure you open on time. Once you pay license fees, get staff on board, and rent an outlet, you incur costs every minute. If you don't start selling and making profits, you bleed money. You can't stop that by coming in late or taking holidays. There is a whole lot of work ahead of you. The fun is in the creation and achievement, and not in some newfound freedom to be lazy.

RELATED TIPS: 35

He works the iPad better than us. Do you think he can email us tips, since he can't speak yet?

A young population makes the field green for early adapters in the consumer B2C market.

It is no secret that the younger generations are the fuel of the social media boom. Social media has made changes not only in business life, but also in political life. The political fabric of entire regions has been altered forever by social media. Former Eastern bloc tactics of media control are no longer applicable within a social media framework. Social media users are now in the billions.

You must have seen three- and four-year-olds playing with an iPad or an iPhone, probably recognizing features their parents have no knowledge of. The younger generation are fast adapters to what's new, what addresses their needs, and what can feed their tremendous desire to share everything with their friends and family. This provides a great opportunity for those who can write new apps or create products to address young people's needs.

Back in 2010, three aspiring young Saudi entrepreneurs had an idea to create an online media channel. They had met at school in Canada and wanted to penetrate new media space with an online media production house. They called their dream Qamariyah; i.e., Lunar. Online media was totally new to the Saudi business culture at the time; the idea of monetizing it was still in its infancy, and probably only a few years old even in the West. Online content space was still evolving, and it continues to do so today. After meeting more than ten prospective investors without much luck, these three young men took their idea to media man Kaswara Al-Khatib. Kaswara, a self-made entrepreneur only a generation older

180

than them, was one of the few Saudis that had penetrated the monopolized media field a few years earlier. After being part of a successful TV show, he started his own media company called FullStop Advertising.

As explained in Tip 70, advertising is one of the fields that has strong monopolies and is very hard to penetrate. Kaswara was one of the young entrepreneurs that dared to try to break in, and he did so successfully. When the three aspiring entrepreneurs approached him, he knew what it meant to start something totally innovative and open a new market. Unlike the other prospective investors, who asked about numbers and track records, and feared risk, he saw an opportunity. He also saw in the entrepreneurs' proposal a prospective business that would complement his offering. They would benefit from his existing infrastructure, a group of media companies that owned expensive filming equipment and studios. His cash investment was limited, but he brought to the table infrastructure that would cost Qamariyah millions to procure on their own. His first step was to rebrand Qamariyah and make it a YouTube channel, not its own proprietary online media channel. The focus of the founding team would be developing content that appealed to the young, Internet-savvy population. When the three young Saudis signed that partnership, granting Kaswara a controlling majority, a star was born, and it was named Uturn. The channel was an instant success, with full return of investment in the first year, an eventual ROI of 700%, and a whopping net growth of 1,500% in three years!!

As mentioned in Tip 10, the young Saudi generation boasts the largest viewership on YouTube per *capita, the second largest percentage of smartphone users in the Middle East, and 29% of the world's tweets; Uturn has managed to capitalize on these numbers, and they have released a number of YouTube programs and channels that are attracting millions of viewers daily. One of these programs has reached two hundred million views on YouTube. Because of their success, they have become an advertising destination for small companies and giants alike. Their programs feature ads from Telco operators, who have been the biggest buyers in mainstream media for a long time. Uturn is a true homegrown Saudi success story, and by itself it manifests most of the tips in this book. This success was demonstrated lately with an investment from France's Five Capital worth $100 million![50]*

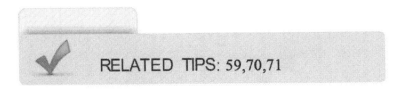

RELATED TIPS: 59,70,71

---

[50] "20 Pacts Worth $18 Billion Signed During Saudi Crown Prince's Visit to Paris," *Saudi Gazette*, July 9, 2018. http://saudigazette.com.sa.

I'm sorry, sir. I clicked on the wrong beneficiary online, and wired the $1M to the company we are suing!

Invest in your staff. The money you save on inefficient employees will be lost in total work inefficiency, and probably in your own medical bills.

Startups are often hungry for cash, and are very cost conscious. Just as you might squander money by making the wrong purchases, which this book has advised against, your extra cautiousness may also lead you to look for savings in the wrong area. Among the areas a startup should invest in carefully is human resource hires.

Bad or inefficient staff can rock a tiny startup boat so hard it could damage or even bankrupt it. If you hire an unqualified person, you will usually end up doing his or her job for him or her. Your time as an entrepreneur is far too valuable to waste on rewriting a bad proposal, performing spell checks, conducting triage after a nasty email to a customer, and so forth. At the same time, hiring someone who is qualified in the wrong area can be devastating to a startup. A big company executive may not be able to function within a cost-conscious, hands-on startup environment.

When we first started expanding IFS Arabia back in the late nineties, we needed to man branch offices. We could not afford (so we thought) expensive employees, so we promoted some of our consultants to managerial positions. Some were up to the challenge, and some failed miserably. Not all of them could handle all aspects of a branch, such as finance, personnel, and administration. Another time, I had an assistant position open up. I interviewed a lady who claimed to know perfect English and passed an interview test. Her first blunder was to use the word "order" instead of "request" with a customer on my behalf. Suddenly, I was "ordering" my customers to send some information! She was fired, and I had to rush to repair the damage, losing time and money. I also was stuck with a number of consultants that were good technically, but could not write proposals. Most of the time, I had to fix their proposals for them. I also had to help some of the pre-sales staff tailor presentations to customers. Not every consultant can smell what the customer needs, and they may wind up filling their presentation with enough information to bore the customer, and maybe lose them. Life changed when I brought in a professional manager from Sweden, who was an ex-IFS AB employee. I promoted him from branch manager to operations manager and had him oversee everything our staff did, from business processes to document and presentation creation, to proposal development. I also hired an ace salesman. It took a lot for me to convince the board that he would be worth his high salary, but he produced a peak in sales in his first year with the company that was greater than any of the years before. Each of these highly qualified employees cost two to three times what my lesser employees had cost, but they were well worth it.

 RELATED TIPS: 57, 58, 60, 64

Knowledge is power.

Competition has an inverse relationship with complexity. If you have some advanced knowledge that is unique, you are going to be more successful and have less competition.

This may sound intuitive, and it goes without saying in the Western world. After all, this is why people make money out of inventions and breakthrough products. Inventing the light bulb made Edison rich. iPhones, iPads, and iPods made Apple reach record high sales.

In the developing world, and in MENA and Saudi Arabia in particular, new technology takes a while to get there, as we saw in related tips. Competition is less fierce, and success depends on introducing a technology first and capturing a market share. Big companies do not move as quickly as a startup does. This is why, for startups, finding something new and bringing it to the region is one of the less risky types of opportunity. Many of the richest families in the region became rich by simply becoming a dealer for a foreign company. Today, dealerships continue to be a good source of income for many startups. I certainly have benefited personally from this with all the companies that I consolidated into the Alcantara Group in 2008.

My second startup was a dealership for an ERP system. In 1996, ERP was new to the MENA region, and we still had to educate the market about it. We were the new kid on the block; the market was dominated by Baan, JDE, and SAP. At the time, Oracle only dealt in financial software, and Microsoft had not bought its way into the market yet. In order to give our product an edge, we became the first to translate it into Arabic. Our competitors used less advanced technology, and localizing products was not as easy for them. IFS used a design that made localization as easy as editing an Apple-like "resource file." I was familiar with this software capability because I had used it to create a multinational visual language for my master's degree at CU Boulder.[51] Thanks to our component-based system files, we were also able to sell the product in smaller pieces, thus appealing to the medium-level market, which could not afford to buy competing products. Five years later, we became one of the largest implementers in the region and increased our revenues by 500% via organic growth only. We also managed to create a set of modules especially for the local market, such as "letter of credit," "zakat" automatic reports, and "Saudi payroll." We enjoyed great success because we introduced new technology while also reading the market's needs. Our R&D was limited, thanks to the one thousand programmers IFS employed to update and upgrade the main product. While they took care of adapting to technology trends and applying them to the application suite, all we did is write local add-ons and small components.

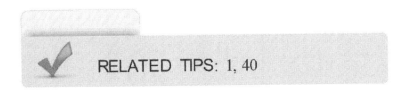

RELATED TIPS: 1, 40

[51] Suleiman, Khalid and Wayne Citrin. "An International Visual Language." Proceedings of the 1992 IEEE Workshop on Visual Languages, Seattle, WA. IEEE Computer Society Press. 1992.

Would you like us to fit any other titles on your business card?

Lack of skilled resources can work to the advantage of young entrepreneurs, who intend to work for their own benefit.

As stated in related tips, sometimes a region suffers from a lack of skilled resources. This is true for many regions even in the US, where skilled programmers are in high demand. This, among other reasons, has led to the outsourcing of programming work to India, the Philippines, and Sri Lanka. However, as much as this is a problem, it can also be an opportunity.

What if the founding team is made up of programmers that are needed to perfect the product? Resources are not always exclusively monetary. The specific knowledge and talent an entrepreneur may have is a resource that can be worth a lot of money. Once you have your prototype, you have already stepped ahead of copycats and competitors. The more you are ahead, the harder it is for them to follow your lead. This type of knowledge has led many great leaders to become what they are today.

Many of the founders of great companies of the day programmed their own prototype systems and used those prototypes to prove the concept, gain traction, and attract investors. Once they had accomplished this, they were able to attract investments that allowed them to hire people to help, but they were always on top of their own craft. Bill Gates was an aspiring young programmer who, with Steve Allen, developed and sold the Altair[52] BASIC programming language, which was popular back in the seventies. Gates's knowledge and his shrewdness landed him the deal with Micro Instrumentation and Telemetry Systems (MITS) that created the ALTAIR. Wozniak was

---

[52] Altair is said to be the twelfth brightest stars in the sky and means "bird" in Arabic.

Steve Jobs's technical sidekick. Without him, the Apple PC would not have seen the light of day, and neither would Apple itself. Larry Page and Sergey Brin, the founders of Google, were two PhD students at Stanford that had something new. Their prototype, which they created as part of their PhD studies, landed them the first $100K angel investment from Andy Bechtolsheim, co-founder of Sun Microsystems. Two of YouTube's three co-founders were computer science graduates who worked for PayPal, and Yahoo's co-founders were electrical engineering graduate students at Stanford. (At the time, computer engineers graduated from electrical engineering departments, as I did). Zuckerberg created the very first version of Facebook in his dorm room. He used a little money from his partners to make it better, but if you've seen the movie The Social Network, or read about this, you know that it was owning the knowledge that made Facebook, not outsourcing. Two other Harvard students, who claimed to have subcontracted Zuckerberg to create a social networking site, ultimately got money in a settlement, but they did not get Facebook—Zuckerberg did. (See the example in Tip 7.)

 RELATED TIPS: 64

Saudi Business Cliché: "Don't try to make profits this time; once we like your work, you will be getting more work from us." Translation: We want more discounts, and we think you're stupid enough to fall for it!

As odd as the above cliché may seem, it is very true, even at very high levels, as demonstrated in the example below. This business cliché is usually used with new smaller suppliers and foreign companies trying to break into the market. Many times the customer has no intention of giving the business any extra work; they just want to get away with more discounts.

Startups are often newcomers to the business, and foreign companies, having a will to penetrate the market and get a good first reference, fall into the trap of opportunistic businessmen. These people know that they will be a potential good reference for you, and they may try to abuse this power to the max. These attempts do not end at signing. Delayed payments can be used to blackmail for extra services, the last installment may be delayed indefinitely, and the extra work may come, but wind up being provided for free at the supplier's expense.

Back in 2004, I was on a special trade mission with HRH Crown Princess Victoria of Sweden, representing IFS AB on a trade delegation to Saudi Arabia. We had a meeting in one of the largest ministries in Saudi, with Ericsson, SAAB, ABB, and other Swedish giants. One of the top executives asked about a multimillion-euro project they had bid for. The minister introduced the famous cliché in the middle of the conversation to encourage the company to offer better prices. Almost every time I have visited a government client with or without a foreign delegate, I have heard the same story. Foreign companies send representatives to Saudi Arabia who are naive to the local culture. They read all sorts of false signals from their

Saudi counterparts. One of my greatest experiences was coaching some of those delegates when I worked as a cross-cultural consultant at MS&B in Boulder, Colorado, back in the early nineties. The course covered a lot of the semantics often misunderstood by foreign expats. Many of the Swedish companies on that delegation had problems with government installments, and were squeezed for a discount. The more prominent ones did not budge and did not take projects that did not make sense to them. The head of a startup asked me once if he should give this huge discount to a large potential reference. I told him that he should not provide the discount unless the customer offered significant added value for him. Sometimes having such a customer as a reference will lead to future projects. In that case it is certainly not a discount, but an investment.

RELATED TIPS: 51, 66

© Khalid Suleimani

A Saudi entrepreneur is like prey swimming in deep waters full of sharks. Be careful; most laws will not protect you.

I was with the former US Ambassador to Saudi Arabia, James Smith, at a dinner at his Riyadh residence on the occasion of the American Independence Day back in 2010. He told me that Saudi Arabia startup culture today is similar to the culture that was prevalent in the USA in the '70s. What he meant is that the SME/startup environment is largely unregulated, allowing the larger companies to monopolize, abuse, crush, and take advantage of small and minority companies. The US has introduced several anti-monopoly laws and laws to protect small and minority business since then, making it hard to "crush" a small business, and giving small businesses access to government projects. The US set-aside program is only one example of how startup culture can change. Since that meeting with the ambassador, I have made it my mission to push for such regulation in Saudi Arabia.

One of the major problems a small business faces in oil-rich Arabia is a lack of access to government projects. These projects require a certain license: a contractor classification, a.k.a. TASNEEF. Getting this certification is impossible without previous experience. How can you get that experience? Well, you have to start off as a subcontractor to one of the big boys. When you do that, however, you open yourself up to a lot of abuse. A large contractor can put ridiculous terms on you, squeeze you, fire you, and drive you out of business. You will get no regulatory protection. The only way to protect yourself is by developing survival techniques.

Back in 2002, IFS Arabia had not gotten the "contractor classification" yet, and we had to work through one of the large system integrators to win a government contract. We had won our first deal with the government, but we could not cite it in the TASNEEF application, because the project was not delivered yet. We learned about a tender that was going to be released by one semi-government agency, which meant that we could apply without a TASNEEF. However, the requirements stated that servers had to be supplied by one of the major hardware suppliers, the largest system integrator in the Kingdom. We started by asking them for a quote, and they offered that we bid for the project jointly. We had a unique offering of a document management system that worked under a Unix flavor they supported. I was suspicious of their intentions and insisted on signing a Memorandum of Understanding (MOU). When the MOU signing was delayed, I became even more suspicious. They kept insisting that we tell them our prices, refusing to supply theirs in accordance with the agreement. The tender deadline was on a Saturday (we used to work Saturdays back then), and it was not until Thursday afternoon, after they had received our prices, that they closed the bid and informed us that they were pulling out and bidding alone!! The whole purpose of the scam had been to learn our prices, nothing more; we posed a threat to their proposed system and had to be neutralized. We could not present a tender ourselves now, because we needed a bank guarantee and that required at least a couple of days. So the Thursday timing was very well planned! Of course I still have the MOU, but who can afford the *time and money for a lawsuit, even if there is enough merit for one?*

RELATED TIPS: 67

I can't take the risk of crossing to you!

Taking risks is an important entrepreneurial trait. If you are not a risk-taker by nature, you may not be able to transform your startup.

I'm not a strong believer that entrepreneurship skills can be acquired. I agree that if you have raw talent, you can help shape it with education, but nobody can teach you the gift of entrepreneurship itself. It's just like being a musician. Sure, you can learn music and write a few tunes, but only the talented will make it. The gift entrepreneurs have is that they see things differently; they see opportunities where others see problems.

Risk should be an entrepreneur's middle name. How else can you go out on a limb to make your startup work? The fuel to staying up long nights, accepting rejection with resolve, and never giving up is the fire of belief in yourself and the ability to take large risks. Those risks can include putting up your savings, quitting your job, taking out a loan against your assets, or trying to fight the big boys with the belief that you can beat them.

In Example 5, we saw how being naive early on can make you lose. In this example, we demonstrate how taking risks continues throughout the life of a venture. Many of the examples in this book have risk written in between the lines. Risk-taking stays with you and has to be there when you need it. As an entrepreneur, I have had to take risks almost every other day. I remember back in 2007, we wanted to demonstrate a pilot of Nexus EMR to the Saudi Arabian Vice Minister of Defense in the annual medical services conference and grand opening. We had to show that we had managed to synchronize medical records between six remote regions. We had all sorts of problems because of security clearances. The hospitals were not linked via the Internet yet, and we wanted to install our own satellite Internet systems.

One week before the event, the servers were stuck in customs, an Internet link had still not been established, and the EMR system was not installed. I talked to the CEO of Nexus, Dr. Ingo Behrendt, who also came from an entrepreneurship background and not a big corporation. Though he had worked for Siemens for years, he had quit to co-found Nexus. We agreed to go ahead with the demonstration. My job was to provide the servers and Intranet twenty-four hours before the event; his job was to get his system to work. After getting all the necessary permits to get the servers out of customs, and getting the satellite team deployed to five locations, I had to deploy my own team to Riyadh, where the main server had to be set up. One of my young Sun engineers took it on his own shoulders to install the Sun servers when our supplier could not meet the tight deadline.

The event was one day away when tight security around an OPEC[53] summit, taking place on the same day in Riyadh, prevented us from driving through the city, where the Nexus system was to be installed on a central server. The team could not get to the central server location before 2:00 p.m., making us lose almost the entire day. A project manager from Nexus called me and tried to stop me from going ahead. I remember telling him it would not hurt to try, and that I would take full responsibility for any failure in front of his boss. On the eve of the event, I took the executives of Nexus, Sun, and Kerfi, who had

---

[53] Organization of the Petroleum Exporting Countries

flown from Sweden, Germany, and the UAE for the event, to a dinner. I could not socialize; I was mainly on my phone getting update texts. Only at 9:30 p.m. did I get the call that the servers and Intranet were ready. I informed Dr. Ingo, who had just arrived and did not attend the dinner. He talked to his guys and started working remotely on the installation. It was not finished until the early morning. We met at 7:00 a.m. at the Intercontinental Ballroom, and I held my breath as the German did the last-minute checking. He gave me a thumbs up! That opening got so much media coverage that we kept using it for years to come.[54,55] It also increased our credibility in front of the customer and sealed our foothold in the project as the small company capable of doing big tasks.

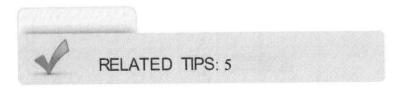

RELATED TIPS: 5

---

[54] Alshihri, Naif. "Conference Explores Ways to Improve Military Hospitals." *Arab News*, April 3, 2007.
[55] "Armed Forces Hospitals Complete Largest Electronic Health System in Saudi Arabia." *News – Healthcare*, December 1, 2008. AMEinfo.com.

But we don't have a tribal head in Switzerland, nor do I know my maternal great, great, great grandfather's name.

The lack of clear laws is a great hindrance to foreign business in Saudi Arabia.

One of the major problems with attracting foreign investment in Saudi Arabia is a lack of clear laws. Saudi Arabia is run on the basis of undocumented laws, which are interpreted on a case-by-case basis by the judge ruling on the case. True, some regulations are written down, particularly those pertaining to commercial enterprises, but for the most part, laws are not written anywhere and are derived directly from religious scriptures. This has led to several cases where two rulings were extremely different even though the cases were almost identical. The country is now undergoing a major law reform, but it will take a while.

It is a common conception of many people in Saudi Arabia that just because something is prohibited, it does NOT mean that you can't legally do it. Sometimes this isn't true—but sometimes it is. *Wasta*—help you get through a personal connection—or *vitamin W* as Saudis like to call it, can alter and bend the rules in your favor. A foreign company wanting to contain its risk may find it very difficult to operate in the Kingdom, though many make it work.

In a relatively recent case, Sepco Electric, a Chinese-American consortium, chose to go public with a dispute with the Minister of Water. The company was bidding for a $3 billion desalination plant in Yanbu and lost to a local company. Sepco believed it was qualified to win and that the standards it tried to meet were not met by the announced winner. It claimed favoritism to a non-qualified local contractor. "[The] Chinese-American consortium asked several government authorities including the National Anti-Corruption Commission and the General

Audit Bureau to investigate why it did not win the contract." [56] This action may seem odd in a fair competition, but the process of seeking government tender accrues lots of costs that are born by the contractor alone. (See the example in Tip 32.) The long tendering process requires visits by experts and a lot of information collection, in addition to the work on the tender itself. Usually, any misinterpretation of the information is the problem of the bidder alone. Therefore, all government contractors go through a long process of due diligence, that in other countries is usually subsidized. Oftentimes the requirements of government tenders are vague and incomplete. They will issue the first tender, learn the about the specs from the bidders, cancel, and reissue. This can drive companies crazy, as their prices get exposed. Many times, we saw our own due diligence and specification included in tenders we applied for that were reissued. When this happens, it does not mean you will win, because the competition may adjust their bids to match yours, and with better prices. The case of Sepco is a clear example of how a lack of clear competition laws can hurt companies, even big ones.

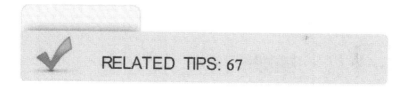

RELATED TIPS: 67

---

[56] "Yanbu Contract: Ministry Rejects Favoritism Claim." *Saudi Gazette*. November 27, 2012. http://www.saudigazette.com.sa.

Stretching the MVP concept: when the media code of business ethics is still in its infancy, it can make you a star overnight!

All it takes sometimes is a gift and a dinner invitation. No, I'm not talking about a date. I'm talking about inviting a reporter to dinner and giving them the gift of a story! This is a common practice in many countries and regions, unfortunately. You can claim you are a designer, a rocket scientist, or even the Messiah, and people will believe you as long as you have a reporter put it in print.

There are many cases where men and women claimed to be international fashion designers, and it became fact as soon as it hit the media. Some of those men and women had nothing to do with fashion design and could barely be classified as tailors. Sometimes their MVP was nothing more than a school project of dolls dressed with stapled rags. Cases like these of media darlings are very common. If you are smart and can deliver on your promises, you can become a star before becoming a real star. However, cashing on an MVP this way is fraud and not a true example of a lean startup.

Some people have stretched these MVP schemes too far. A few years ago, researchers in one university claimed they had created a prototype of the first Saudi car. It was all over the news, and the credibility of the researchers was not questioned, since the president of the university was championing them. The media took off with the story, but when people started asking questions about what was unique about this car, the answers were vague. Surely you can't "invent" a car, because cars have already been invented. You have to patent something about a car that makes it unique. It turned out that the car in question was assembled from Korean parts, and looked exactly like the Korean car which they had borrowed the body parts from. So where was the invention? After much public scrutiny, it turned out they had filed for a "camel bumper" patent. But even that turned out to be patented to another company in Australia! One year after this story—a clear case of abusing both the MVP and media immaturity—broke, the scam was revealed and the president of the university was sacked in shame. Unfortunately, some startups get away with manipulating the primitive state of local mainstream media reporters, but in the age of social media, you will be busted as soon as you release your MVP, which is not actually an MVP.

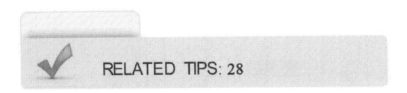

RELATED TIPS: 28

Objecting to zakat and tax bills may have undesirable consequences.

In Saudi Arabia, businesses enjoy minimal or no taxes. However, some businesspeople object to any type of tax enforced by the Department of Zakat and income tax. The only form of tax paid is 2.5% "zakat" per year on earnings retained for over a year, per Islamic law. Saudi Arabia used to enforce income tax on expats, but it does not do so anymore. However, it started placing heavy fees on expats and their families in 2017. There is a tax of 20% on profits made by foreign investment companies, and also on income made by foreign service companies operating in the Kingdom via dealers. As part of the financial offset program introduced by Vision 2030, customs charges, which were almost zero, will gradually be put back. A special sin tax on harmful goods was introduced, and VAT came into effect starting 2018. Each company, including startups, would have to have a specialized tax auditor, like all other companies in the world.

If you're a startup, it is not wise to object to your tax statement unless you see a really major miscalculation. Otherwise, your friends in the tax department will try to dig into your books and find a reason to tax you more. For some reason, the guys over there feel you are enjoying an almost tax-free status, so you might as well shut the hell up and pay!!

In the early days of my startups, I was new to the idea of business taxation in Saudi Arabia. Like any other entrepreneur, I was very keen to save any penny I could. I got a tax audit once, and it read around $20K. I went berserk; that was too much for us. So we objected. After six months of negotiations and the withholding of our tax certificate (which was necessary to get many government operations done and payments released), the charge was reduced by half. However, we were audited for the preceding five years, and it turned out that suddenly the annual dealership fee we used to pay our foreign partner was also taxable. I had to pay five years in back taxes thanks to the stupid objection. Ultimately, I'm pretty sure I paid more than $20K the second time around. Many of my colleagues have had similar experiences. My advice: think twice before objecting. In many countries tax agencies are despised, and their employees, who are only doing their jobs, are also generally hated. They have overwhelming power, so don't mess with them.

RELATED TIPS: 69

Chapter 4

The Growth Stage

In this stage, startups seek scaling and attempt to achieve high growth. This is where marketing activities need to be shifted into a repeatable process that is easy to replicate for multiple sales. This is a very important stage in the life of a startup, which will determine whether it can win extra funding from VCs or not.

Key Activities: In this stage, the venture starts taking the form of a real business, with larger customer acquisition, back-end scalability improvements, the first executive hires, process implementation, and establishment of departments as in a normal business.

Funding Type: Multiple rounds of VC financing, referred to as rounds A, B, C, D, E, F... and so on, as required until reaching the IPO or acquisition stage.

He's been following that bounced check for the past 7 years.

A bounced check is almost always a sign that you have lost your money for a long while, if not forever.

This is particularly true in Saudi Arabia. Other MENA countries, even the poorest ones, such as Egypt, Morocco, and Jordan, have strong laws against bouncing a check. You can take the person who gave you the bad check to jail almost immediately. In Saudi Arabia, this is not the case. Sure, laws have improved and have made this a serious offense leading to public humiliation, but the laws are not enough.

In most cases, you will have to take your debtor to court. This means years of deliberations before a ruling, and at least a year of appeals afterward. Recently, this has become a specialty of commercial courts. Even if you get a positive ruling, say, two years later, you still have to wait for the ruling to be executed. These delays are rarely affordable for a small business or a startup. A bounced check can put them out of business. To avoid problems, check your check issuer's credit report; only accept cashier's checks or direct deposits of cash to avoid risks.

The laws against bouncing checks have been there for a long time, but the execution of those laws is still in its early stages. Sure, you can file a court case and start litigating, but the process will take a long time. It was only in March 2013 that a law was finally put in place to allow you to take a bounced check along with a bank letter describing the incident to the execution judge directly.[57] The introduction of this law has caused execution courts bounced check cases to increase to 108 cases per day.[58]

---

[57] "Riyadh Al-Almaee Reporting," *Alyoum Daily*, March 2, 2013.
[58] "*mahakim altaneez tanner 108 Qadaya shaik murtaja3 yawmiya*," *Tawasul* electric paper, March 5th, 2017.

214

However, the severity of this problem is demonstrated in the Saudi credit bureau (Simah) annual report[59], which states that the number of bounced checks in the country was down in 2012 to 44,984 checks, with a value of around $1 billion, compared to 167,155 checks with a value of $4 billion in 2009. This shows a significant improvement, but it also demonstrates the extent of the problem that still exists. It is expected that with the new laws in place, this phenomenon will continue to decline, given that credit reports are now available to most businesses. A negative credit rating due to a bounced check will help a startup assess whether to accept a check or not. Courts are filled with cases of people who sold pieces of land or other goods and got a check that bounced. Some people sold their houses and got a delayed check that was never backed by any cash. To many people, this can mean losing their life savings. Therefore, most people do not trust personal checks and prefer either cash or cashier's checks.

RELATED TIPS: 53

---

[59] www.SIMAH.com

A rumor-spreading employee is like a disease-spreading virus. Get rid of them at any cost.

Among the things that you can never learn about an employee from a resume or an interview are their personal traits. As in any relationship, some things can only be learned when you have dealt with someone in person for a while. Some employees are lazy, full of excuses, avoid taking responsibility, and are not team players. But those traits are local to the employee, though they may spread on a limited level. The trait of rumor-spreading can create damage throughout your organization, making it the worst employee flaw of all.

My advice: if you find an employee that enjoys spreading rumors, get rid of them. They are destructive to your small or even large company or department. Some of these rumors are malicious, thus causing wide resentment within the staff, and can distract your company if they are not dealt with. You don't want to spend your time denying rumors; most of the time, people will not believe you anyway, and in any case, this will do little to contain any damage that has already been done.

I hired a marketing manager back in late 2010. She had a great resume, with just the right qualifications. She showed great personality in the interview, so I hired her. A few weeks into the job, she started accusing someone in the administration of harassing her. This was a serious accusation, and firing that guy meant we would lose a great asset. But I looked into it, and after a long series of investigations and questions that wasted time and energy, it turned out that the poor guy, who was loved by everyone else, had not harassed her. All he did was ask her to prove a certain expense, as per company policy. She took it as a personal attempt by him to stop her from getting her expenses refunded, and she spread her rumor in retaliation. Another guy who worked for me at IFS Arabia, who was a superb programmer, had the habit of spreading rumors to his colleagues. Among the most vicious rumors he spread was that certain staff members were favored and got more benefits than others. This hit two of his peers particularly hard. It took us years to discover that the reason behind certain staff members leaving us was his malicious rumors. When we did figure it out, we eventually fired him, after warning him many times. Losing him was hard for the technical team, but we had to cut our losses.

RELATED TIPS: 47

58

Now you truly represent all of us in front of the customer.

Carefully handpick staff that represent you in front of your customer, and filter everything that goes out to clients. Sometimes you get no second chances.

Many of the companies I started were B2B businesses. We worked very closely with a number of customers, and could not afford to lose them. That meant we had to write proposals and do presentations that were customer specific. It also meant that our consultants, pre-sales, and sales staff always had to look their best.

In a startup, you can never afford to lose any customers, whether you are B2B or B2C. But if you are a young startup and have only a few first customers, losing any of them can be a disaster. A bad presentation, a bad proposal, or an arrogant comment to one of the customer's employees can be very hard to fix. You should really coach and mentor your staff on how to deal with customers, and you should be ready to absorb angry calls and smooth things out with your client. If it turns out that some of your staff don't have good people skills, move them to backstage jobs, or get rid of them.

As stated in related tips, a presentation is always a show. You have to engage the audience and know where to place your punch lines. The same goes for all types of customer communications. A key to all of your communications is being able to understand your customer. Tell them what they want to hear, and carefully craft the message you want to send. This not only goes for sales, but also for consulting and systems implementation. The staff you send to your customers represent you. Not only do they have to look good, but they have to be coached in interpersonal communication skills. When Alcantara worked with the Ministry of Defense medical services, we had to hire lots of new staff and work with teams of Germans and Swedes, in addition to our local staff. We first had to align each of our staff members with their mates and then coach our European colleagues on how to deal with the Saudi government. European staff take any comment from anyone who claims to be a mover and shaker seriously. Many updates they made to the system were suggestions that were not approved by their superiors. They wanted to make the customer happy, but I needed to control costs and make sure that the person that wrote the check was happy. Trying to keep the customers, the staff, and the generals happy all at the same time was not easy.

RELATED TIPS: 33, 47

I've hit the glass ceiling so many times, I use Windex for hairspray now

Doing business sometimes means avoiding hitting the glass ceiling that separates the men from the boys!

Anyone with some experience dealing in Saudi Arabia knows that there are glass ceilings that a startup will hit when trying to penetrate the market. There is not just one glass ceiling, but several that separate the layers of business in Saudi Arabia. This particularly pertains to B2B. B2C also suffers from market leaders who can use indirect means to pressure them and put them out of business. But in general, startups dealing directly with consumers will run into fewer problems with market entry, because no one can prevent you from opening up your own retail business and selling directly to your customers.

Knowing your capabilities, being aware of glass ceilings, and watching out for monopolists is important when you are establishing your business plan, and it will help you to set reasonable targets. Moving past the glass ceilings is hard, but not impossible, as the cases of Uturn and Yahya, described in related tips, prove. It's always how you get your first set of projects that defines whether you can play in a certain league or not. Once you have your first set of projects in some league, you can get other projects on your own. Not being able or not knowing how to land those first projects means losses for years in potential sales, even if you have the best offering around.

Think of these leagues as ones you need to qualify to "play" in. Connections are the main ticket to play, but turnover will help you measure whether you can play with bigger boys or not. For the Champions league, you'll need a minimum of $150 million in turnover; Premier: $30 million; First: $7 million; Second: $2 million. For higher leagues, it's almost impossible to play if another member does not endorse you, either by offering you a first contract or by giving you a subcontract. Once you gain the trust of the league members, they may or may not let you play along. Some startups accomplish this by partnering with someone from the league they want to gain access to. Be careful though; these shrewd businessmen, if they agree to give you a chance, may take advantage of you. Most of them will not agree to a profit share or a commission against projects, but will require a high equity share in your startup. Some of them will make sure that you never play.

A young entrepreneur created a Little League soccer club for kids under ten. He was struggling with getting a license. One of his potential investors demanded more than 50% of his club in exchange for getting him a very hard-to-get license—in fact, no such license exists yet. The entrepreneur was afraid that if he lost a majority share, he would be disposed of later. Negotiations still go on in the absence of an official license. He is under the constant threat of being shut down at any time, and there was no hope of scaling in the absence of a valid license, until July 2017. That month, licensing laws for small hobby clubs were finally introduced allowing this entrepreneur and others to operate under the license of the new General Sports Authority (GSA), another Vision 2030 fruit. This license finally put this entrepreneur in the power seat in front of investors. He also may be getting more support from *a program for developing sports and hobby clubs led by the Quality of Life VRP, to be launched soon.*[60]

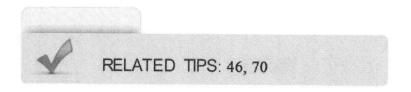

RELATED TIPS: 46, 70

---

[60] Quality of Life Delivery Plan (2018-2020), March 2018. pp. 68.

If you are an innovative or even a service company, your staff is your most valuable asset. Minor overstaffing can provide crucial insurance.

When you are a small organization with a small number of key personnel, losing even one of your employees can be disastrous to your existence. In countries with abundant resources, some of these employees may be easily replaced. However, if the person you have lost holds expertise that is key to your business, then it might take a considerable amount of time to replace him or her. To prevent a staffing disaster, you need insurance.

This tip can apply to any company in any country at certain times. Nowhere in the world are all types of resources available ALL the time. For certain types of businesses, certain functions require certain skill sets that may not be readily available or may require a knowledge transfer. This transfer can take place via formal training, on-the-job training, or handover from other staff. In all of these cases, the staff member holding the critical knowledge cannot be let go overnight. If they are, it will pose a major threat to the business's stability.

When I worked as the managing director of my second startup, IFS Arabia, back in 1997, our business depended considerably on consultants who implemented the Swedish ERP software. These consultants did not come from Saudi, where resources were scarce, but from Europe, Asia, and the Middle East. It took us at least six months of training and on-project experience to start getting a benefit out of each one of them. We started small, so one consultant would cover more than one area. Our software had around eight application areas, including finance, manufacturing, human resources, customer relationship management (CRM), distribution, and so on. Whenever one of our consultants got a better offer or resigned, the business suffered a lot. With time, I learned to keep at least a 25% spare capacity of consultants ready to take over if any of their colleagues left. It cost me more, but it gave me a lot of comfort in running the business. If your business depends on resources that are not easily replaceable, try to do the same. In Saudi, headhunting can take up to six months. If you go with foreign workers, then work permits will be a pain. And if your new hires need to be local, it's even more painful, as their original employers are rarely willing to let them go. Consider the factors in your local environment and take precautions, or, as we put it in this tip, get insurance!

RELATED TIPS: 61, 64

Till bankruptcy do us apart.

Pick your staff to stay; firing staff in most countries is hard and can be very expensive.

Labor laws were designed mainly to protect employees' rights, not employers' rights. This policy dates from the days when unions first stood up to fight for the rights of employees. This is particularly true in Socialist Europe and is also true in Saudi Arabia. Saudi's labor laws were revised more than one time during the past few years. However, at the moment, if an employee's contract exceeds its original period, or automatic renewals adding up to four years, and neither party notifies the other otherwise, the contract becomes "indefinite." This is when troubles start for an employer. The articles stipulating the right to fire an employee make this very difficult unless there has been a major offense perpetrated by the employee against the employer, such as leaking trade secrets, fraud, embezzlement or continuous absence from work. These situations usually go under article 80.[61] Otherwise, the employer has to pay compensation to the employee, which can be up to six-month salaries.

Problems can arise if the company needs to downsize or pivot, or for any other reason finds an employee superfluous or unfit for the job. These situations are not covered by labor laws. If an employee is fired, he has the right to sue in the labor court. Lawsuits take time, but once a ruling takes place, it can require you to put the employee back on the job, which typically includes back pay of all salaries for the absence period. Many companies choose to settle with an employee by paying him six months' to a year's salary, plus end-of-service pay, which can be up to one month's salary for each year of previous service.

---

[61] "Saudi Labor Law." Royal Decree No. M/46, 26-3-2015.

There are many examples of labor law abuse on both the employee's and the employer's side. What usually happens from the employer's side is that they try to make the working conditions hard on the employee, forcing him or her to quit voluntarily. Even in that case, the employee can sue, claiming the employer made his job difficult. But some tactics used by employers depend on degrading the employee in subtle ways that make their life difficult. For example, an employee might be transferred to a remote location, have his title changed, be demoted, or be given the worst office in the building. Employees who sue in these circumstances usually get either a very handsome compensation package or get reinstated. This can be an employer's worst nightmare, because it often means paying years of back salaries from the day employment was terminated. There are cases where a group of "downsized" employees sued a company and were reinstated two or three years later, and the employer had to pay their salaries for the whole period. Not paying means the government can shut down all the company's services, such as work permits, licenses, and so forth, making it hard for the business to operate.

 RELATED TIPS: 60

Startup employee payday is a happy day for everyone but the entrepreneur, who does all the paying and rarely pays himself.

In the beginning, a startup works with limited funds from seeds or angels. Once it starts making sales, it gradually starts depending on itself to sustain its operations. This period is the hardest for the entrepreneur, due to the fragile nature of the business and the uncertainties surrounding its operations.

One of the major bills to be paid every month is staff salaries. Payday is a nightmare to the owner(s). The business is often still not making enough cash or is running on limited financing. A lot has to be purchased, with low income projected for many months ahead, and the bottom lines all red. These are only some of the thoughts that will go through your mind as you pay your staff. On top of this, during this period, you will rarely pay yourself—and you might even be paying your employees' checks from your own pocket just to keep the business going for another month.

For many years, the end of the month was a nightmare to me. Our first set of customers was taking a risk working with us instead of our well-established competitors. This meant that they often abused payment terms for no reason, or asked for extra services. We did not have cash reserves, and it was hard to replace those customers who paid eventually. But until they did, it was tough. We could not get bank financing either, so we had to work very hard to make the end-of-the-month bills. When you're selling new technology, you have the burden of educating your customer, sometimes at the expense of timely payments. Spend your money wisely, hire rationally, and deal with your customers with care. For us, working on building cash reserves and operating within very tight budgets was the only way we could cope with the situation.

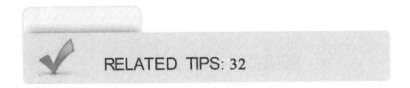

RELATED TIPS: 32

Spending most of your time putting out fires will hinder your startup's growth and your innovation. Get good help or you'll never grow.

The most valuable asset to your startup is you. You are the main engineer, the top salesman, the guru marketer, and the phantom behind the machine. If you are going to involve yourself in the stupid details, then you will have less time to focus on the stuff that no one else can do.

Small operational problems are a daily routine of every business, from paying a late phone bill to chasing a late package, to filling out some bureaucratic form, to attending to a customer problem. Most of these small problems can be handled by efficient staff. If you think you are saving money by doing this stuff yourself, then you are wrong. Your man-hours are worth a lot more than those of the person you would hire to do this stuff. So unless you can do nothing for your business, get some good help and focus on making money.

Back in 1996, I took on a project to salvage a failing company. When I took over, it had all sorts of problems: understaffing, underfunding, and under-qualification of engineers. The owner had helped the company get a couple of deals signed for Avalon ERP's new GUI version; however, none of the staff was trained to work with the new product. It was a hot summer in 1996. I had to have the staff qualified before the scheduled start of the projects. A minor glitch in the customer system, plus the summer break, gave me an extra window of a few weeks to make sure I could make the implementation. Losing the customer would have been a disaster, as we had already collected down payments. At that point, my role as the head was simply to put out fires. It was only a few years later, after the company, which I eventually bought, stabilized, that I could focus on its growth. Life was harder at that time, without the Internet, email, or mobile phones.

In Appendix 4 is a timeline for the events from the summer of 1996 of the nerve-wracking period that preceded getting the staff trained on August 26th. We went through an ordeal battling the absence of technical staff from our and Avalon's side. In addition, our company had tons of internal problems, let alone the problems Avalon itself was facing, which ended with it declaring bankruptcy by the end of the summer. Communicating with the West was harder at the time due to our Thursday/Friday weekend. This meant we had only 3.5 days of communication per business week.

The events described in the timeline may not concern the reader per se. However, they demonstrate what "putting out fires" means for a business in concrete terms. They also demonstrate how an entrepreneur must face all the hurdles and risks no matter what to achieve his or her goal. If you try hard and give it your best, then either you enjoy a win, or at least you can't blame yourself if you fail, and this is exactly what happened that summer. At one point we were about to give up and lose our credibility, the training, and the money we got from clients, but we never gave up. As a result, we managed to pull it off and score a win with our clients.

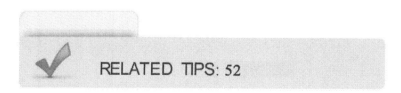

RELATED TIPS: 52

He finally got these visas, but his heart could not take it.

Getting a visa for an expat from the Saudi Labor Office is so hard for a startup. The day you finally get one should be a holiday to add to Eid and National Day.

As explained in related tips, local talent is almost impossible to find. And if you do manage to find somebody you want, they will not work for a startup. This has caused the word *visa* become associated with something very precious. Labor from poor Asian countries used to pay up to $5K to buy a black-market visa to the Kingdom. Those visas bypassed the normal procedure of checking quotas and qualifications for labor. The practice was abolished in 2013, and all illegal labor was extradited in a correction campaign that affected more than five million people out of the nine million foreign workers in the country.[62]

The process of getting a work permit is very complex, as the country is currently trying to limit the influx of foreign workers, which topped nine million in 2013. Several measures have been imposed to discourage companies from relying on foreign workers, particularly cheap Asian and African labor. The Ministry of Labor has pushed for tough measures to make sure businesses rely on automation, the local workforce, and other means, rather than depending on a cheap workforce that is flooding the country. Unfortunately, these regulations are blind and make it impossible to get work permits for the staff you need. Therefore, when a company gets a work permit, it's usually a reason to celebrate.

The story I'm about to tell you is not fiction. It actually took me seven years to get our first work permit "officially." Of course, we had to use other means; without a workforce, we would not have survived. Back in 1997,

---

[62] AFP Arabic, News, November 5, 2013. http://www.afp.com/ar/node/1148289/.

when we bought the company that became IFS Arabia, we needed ERP consultants, so we opened a file at the Labor Office. The process finally ended in 2004 with us receiving five visas. Opening the labor file required tons of copies of every single registration, and two very important certificates: a tax or zakat certificate, and a GOSI (social security) certificate. The first guarantees that you have paid your taxes, and the second shows that you have paid social insurance for your staff. So far, this seems normal. However, it takes up to a year to get your zakat certificate, because they have to look at your current audited statement. The issued certificate expires after six months. The GOSI certificate requires the zakat certificate to be issued, and the labor office requires both to be current. We could not get these three moons to line up on the same axis until our seventh year of trying. And a lucky seven it was indeed! The good news is that GOSI is now issued online, and a zakat certificate takes much less time to be issued. However, the Labor Office has made it harder to receive work permits than ever before. Another solution, offered by the Ministry of Labor, is to hire labor for SMEs from other SMEs via an online portal named Ajeer.

Best Business Plan
Competition

My idea was to resell recycled government green folders.
The estimated returns are enough to pay for the US
national debt.

A "government facilitator" is the cure to most Saudi bureaucratic illnesses.

Saudi Arabia is an interesting place to start a business, in addition to a lack of clear rules and the problems government employees add to the already complex bureaucracy.

Anyone who has dealt with Saudi Government entities before knows that he has to carry the infamous "Green Hanging Folder" including photocopies of his ID, CR, and COC. The moment he gets to his destination, new requirements arise and the real party starts. As sad as it may sound, it is rare to find anyone in the Saudi Government who can give you a clear set of regulations for carrying out a certain transaction. Even if you download the requirements from the official website of the government agency you are dealing with, there is almost certainly something missing.

That "something" is known only to the government worker you are dealing with. It might also change from one worker to another, one city to another, or even one neighborhood to another if you are dealing with a municipality or a police station. Depending on the mode of the public servant, your papers maybe deemed incomplete, even they actually weren't. It is next to impossible to argue, because the "government" the public servant represents is always right, and if anyone is wrong, it has to be you, the citizen. Even when you finally hand in your complete big fat folder, the worker will audit it in his own unique way and find out something is missing. That something may be a document that has expired, or a document that has never been mentioned in a website, verbally by the same worker, or in the official literature.

When that happens, you may have to redo everything again and take a tour office to office, going to appointment after appointment, no matter how far apart. The "Green Hanging Folder" has become a symbol of Saudi bureaucracy. I don't know who makes them, but I'm sure he is a very rich man.

Therefore, you really can't get around government offices without a so-called *muaqib* or "government facilitator" who was enforced upon companies and private enterprises by the government for a long time. A government facilitator is someone who either has a connection to an existing or an ex-employee, or is one himself. Use one, or his friends at the organization he is connected to will make sure you suffer, and you may never get your work done.

I should mention, however, that these problems are almost nonexistent in government offices that have developed e-services, and they are diminishing in some others. Different e-government iterations made many government entities agree on unified measures for dealing with citizens. The introduction of e-government services has standardized the system considerably. Even so, at the present day, some ministries are still more advanced than others. The Ministry of the Interior is a leader and is pushing the whole government structure forward. The Ministries of Labor, Commerce, and Justice are following. The PKI (public key identifier) infrastructure is complete, and single sign-ons (SSO) are available for most government services. PKI and SSO facilitate the access to many government sites with the same unified MOI credentials. Still, the fight between electronic and paper-based procedures goes on, and thousands of such facilitators' lives depend on it. Those have started finding other lines of work, including dealing with the complexity of e-services for the computer illiterate or those who are too lazy to do it themselves.

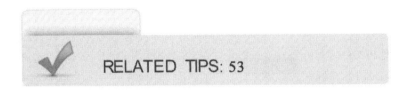

RELATED TIPS: 53

The final installment is a myth; everyone talks about it, but rarely does a subcontractor see it. Always make sure that you can make profits in its absence.

One of the not-so-good business practices in Saudi Arabia is delaying supplier payments. If you are a startup or an SME, this process can kill you, because any disruption in your cash flow can be painful. The practice started in the mid-'80s, when oil prices went down to $8 a barrel. National income went down to the extent that the government had to borrow money for the first time. One of the symptoms of the economic problem, which lasted for over twenty years, was that the government itself delayed its supplier and contractor payments.

This practice, in a country where 90% of income is oil-related, meant that the main source of cash throughout the nation was delayed. This reflected on larger suppliers, who delayed money to their subcontractors, and so on down to the little guy. Bounced checks did not carry any major punishment, at least in practice, nor did un-honored IOUs. Even today, when government payments take no more than a few weeks and all supplier payments are made by direct wire transfer, some of the suppliers find this a hard habit to shake. Some pay all installments late, and in particular, the last installment is like some mystical creature that you hear about in fairy tales. We have all heard about the last installment, but rarely have we seen, touched, or felt it. The customer simply finds an excuse not to pay it.

My companies were not alone in having their bills two or three years overdue. Usually, the customer finds an excuse not to pay the last installment. The best practice for a supplier is to get money based on milestones and make sure that not paying will compromise the project if those milestones are not met. Also, try to make sure that the final acceptance installment is as small as possible. In your books, be prepared to write off these final installments, because the chances you will get them are 50/50 on a good project. Companies find all sorts of creative ways to get their money. They may go as far as stopping service to their customers. As damaging as this practice can be to the client-supplier relationship, sometimes it's just absolutely necessary. Some companies lose their accounts if they do this, but some just blame it on the foreign supplier. We used to blame the Swedes at IFS for almost everything in front of our customers. Otherwise, we would look as arrogant as the suppliers! The Swedes were understanding, but sometimes it was just impossible not to pay them. It would be a tough decision to jeopardize the dealership for the sake of an abusive customer.

RELATED TIPS: 50, 56, 80

We would like to renegotiate the payment terms on our contract.

Contracts may only be enforceable through lengthy lawsuits. Therefore, most startups choose to protect themselves with guerrilla tactics.

As we discussed in related tips, knowing the playing field is important to your ability to score a goal. One of the major problems that hinders business in many countries is related to law enforcement. Companies, startups, and entrepreneurs are (understandably!) reluctant to start a business in a country they are not sure will protect their rights.

In most countries, whether laws are enforceable or not, suing someone is a lengthy and costly process. In the US, for example, lawsuits can be expensive for a small business, even though the law is highly enforceable through the court systems. In a country like Saudi Arabia, laws are not necessarily easily enforceable, but guerrilla tactics can help you get your money back. This process can be cheaper than suing in another country.

Being in a country such as Saudi Arabia, where lawsuits are lengthy and can take years or where the laws are simply unclear, has forced many startups to use guerrilla tactics to protect themselves. This can make doing business particularly hard. Most startups try to link their payments with milestones that may be hidden to the customer. For example, they may delay a certain delivery until the due payment is made. Sometimes they have to go to the customer and complain that life is tough and that they need their help with the installment. I know it sounds absurd to "beg" for your rights, but some customers will get offended if you "demand" your rights.

Conversely, sometimes a customer will ask a startup for a bank guarantee against a down payment. This happened to me in the early days. The customer did not know us, and we seemed too small, and they felt they were taking a risk giving us the deal. So they asked for a bank guarantee against the first installment. Once we started delivering, the relationship eased up and they started paying more without guarantees. In other words, the customer's business was protecting itself against a supplier (us) via a bank guarantee. This would not have happened had they known that they could protect their investments via the courts.

Unfortunately, this story has a second part, in which it was the customer that was the offender, not us. This customer suddenly decided he did not want an expensive ERP, so he canceled our contract after final delivery. Not only did he do that, but he kept asking for more changes, threatening to liquidate the initial payment bank guarantee. When I had finally had it with them and insisted on being paid, not only did they cancel the contract, but they liquidated the guarantee too. I sued. It took seven years for us to win, and get a ruling for full compensation— interest-free, of course.[63] It turns out that the customer had a whole department handling lawsuits from his suppliers, whom he never paid. That was his finance technique: hold payments, let them sue you, and enjoy free finances for five to seven years, depending on the date of the ruling, if not forever.

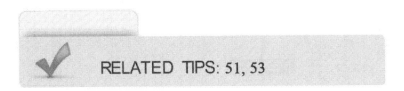

RELATED TIPS: 51, 53

---

[63] In Saudi Arabia, you cannot ask for interest compensation in a lawsuit due to conflict with religious laws.

68 TIP

Demo Day

...And after reading to you our program code to you, Zack will sing it for you.

In a sales pitch, don't "sell" what you think is technically valuable about your product only. Place most of your focus on the need you are fulfilling for your customers.

Many entrepreneurs are engineers or programmers in love with their product and its features, and they take every occasion to talk about it just like a proud dad. This is good only if it leads to perfecting the product to meet customer needs. It's not good if no one else cares but you.

Customers and investors alike care about the benefits your product can bring them. What will the product deliver to them; how much money or time will it save them; how does it compare to the products of your competitors; how is it an improvement over older technology? Neither really cares about the details of the technology itself beyond its use and benefits. You don't want to bore your clients, so only tell them what they really want to know.

Americans are masters of marketing, and when you work with other countries, you can see the difference. I was invited to a partner conference of IFS, the Swedish ERP developer, back in 2002 in Gothenburg, Sweden. For two days, I saw all sorts of presentations about technology—how they developed it, how they did configuration management, and how versions were rolled out. What? A sales conference with not a single presentation on how to sell, business cases, selling points and techniques, marketing tips, or guidelines for marketing communication? Except for a one-hour presentation on the afternoon of the last day, when most people were ready to catch their flights, no information on sales was presented during the conference.

IFS was a company made up of engineers and was run by a founder who was very proud. But pride does not sell. Many entrepreneurs are so proud of their technical achievements that they forget to sell their product. When in a presentation, think like a salesman and not like a developer. A couple of years after that IFS conference, I attended a PeopleSoft partner conference in Amsterdam. No one talked about product technicalities. The whole conference was about sales cases, presentations by real salespeople, and marketing strategies. A year later, PeopleSoft was acquired by Oracle, as it was one of the most successful competitors in its field. That resulted in sales plummeting, and the board decided to sack the founder CEO and appointed the head of IFS UK, which was one of the highest selling regions among other IFS country offices, and he stills runs the company at the time of printing this edition. PeopleSoft was acquired by Oracle in 2004 and went on to become the leading ERP player, while IFS, who had its eye on that deal, became a niche player and never made it to the big boys' club.

RELATED TIPS: 33, 82

Foreign withholding tax collection.

Outsourcing services to foreign companies carries a tax of 20% in KSA. Be careful; your startup will be exclusively liable to pay at your tax review.

This is one of the Saudi regulations that entrepreneurs do not discover until it's too late; i.e., at tax audit time. The danger behind this regulation is that even if the tax is paid by the foreign company, giving their local contractor or dealer the comfort of thinking they are not liable, the local dealer is the one responsible in front of authorities.

Many startups in the MENA region in general, and Saudi Arabia in particular, depend on outsourcing their services to foreign expertise. This is particularly true for consulting, programming, and training. All these services, if outsourced to a foreign company and billed locally, are subject to a withholding tax (WHT) of up to 20%. Many startups realize this only after the service is billed and delivered and the foreign company is paid, without withholding the tax amount payable to the tax authority, which should be reported every three months for SMEs and every month for larger companies.[64] Objecting on the grounds that you "didn't know" is not acceptable. Pay, or suffer the consequences from the guys at the zakat and the income bureau.

When I got my big-break deal in Alcantara with the Ministry of Defense back in 2007,[65] we were carrying out the project with a "dream team" of four foreign companies: IFS, Nexus, Sun, and Oracle, each of whom we represented and subcontracted to. This meant that we would lose 20% of our income to WHT. I had to look into ways to reduce that tax so I could maximize our profits.

[64] Article 63 of Saudi Income Tax code, based on decree (1535) of the minister of finance, published in *Umm Al-Qura* paper issue (4102), dated 27-5-1427H.
[65] "Saudi Arabian Information Technology Report Q1, 2010." *Business Monitor International*, January 2010.

Tax and customs charges on sold goods were zero, but services were taxable. "Services" included all implementation work, so training and consulting had to be dealt with. Such services comprised more than half of the project value. The best option was actually to implement the project using local staff. This could only be done if our staff was familiar with the products. But even with the IFS team I had, I was understaffed. I had to make sure that I hired and trained new staff at Sun, Oracle, and IFS, and I was put up against the delivery deadlines in the project plan. For some of my subcontractors, this meant meeting tight deadlines, and for others it was more relaxed.

The larger problems were with the Nexus EMR software. This technology was new to us; we had recently been appointed as the exclusive dealer, and we needed dozens of newly trained staff. That was simply not feasible with the time constraints. (See Tip 64.) The only way around outsourcing this work to Nexus was to create a joint venture with them. This meant that they got a good presence in Saudi, easier access to work permits, and a good platform for future projects in the Middle East. For me, it meant a vehicle for qualifying local staff, and a reduction of the foreign tax by more than half. A mixed nationality joint venture only pays 20% of the "profits" of the foreign partner. This meant that resource expenses were deducted from the profits, which was a major improvement over the 20% flat fee on "revenue" I would have to pay if they were subcontracted by Alcantara, the prime contractor. It also meant that my company would be liable for none of the taxes, since the tax would be paid on the profits of the foreign partner alone, which had established a legal presence in Saudi and would be solely liable to pay to the Department of Zakat and Income Tax.

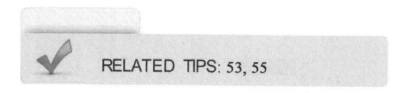

RELATED TIPS: 53, 55

Let me get this right: To join the "family," I have to kill the competition?

There are a handful of monopolists in every sector. If you can't beat them, join them.

Market leaders sometimes have enough market shares to put off any new startup from attempting to take them over. This is particularly true for countries where anti-monopoly laws are not in place. However, even in countries with no monopolies, big companies will try to buy potentially threatening little companies if they can't crush them.

In Saudi Arabia, where there is little or no clear law against monopoly, it can be very hard for a startup to take a considerable piece of a monopolist's market share. The big guy can simply flex his muscles and drive you out of business. Big boys are sometimes involved in cartels that prevent newcomers from joining. There is no law against cartels in Saudi Arabia, and no anti-monopoly regulations. The government has intervened in certain cases when basic food prices rose due to cartels. On some other occasions, consumers started campaigns to boycott certain goods, such as milk and chicken, to pressure suppliers.[66] But there are no regulatory bodies monitoring monopolies, nor any clear penalties so far.

In Saudi Arabia, the market is dominated by family businesses. Big family businesses have common ties and shared interests. Most markets have been divided between such families for a long time. The big guys do not invade each other's "territories," but they may join forces to drive out a considerable threat to their respective monopolies. However, a lot of new startups have created new markets in recent years. Those are the people who are not afraid and will not be intimidated by stronger

---

[66] "Campaign Urges Saudi Chicken Boycott Over Price Rises." *BBC News Middle East*, October 5, 2012.

market leaders. In the example that accompanies Tip 46, I discussed Uturn and how the founders managed to penetrate a media monopoly by using a new medium. In the present example, we follow a group of new designers who changed the way men dress in Saudi Arabia, pushing out a group of traditional tailors who had previously dominated the market.

In 1994, I met Yahya, an aspiring young fashion designer, when we did a workflow study for his fashion factory, which he wanted modernized. He had completed his fashion studies in Paris a few years earlier and had made it as a successful women's haute couture designer. He had dressed celebrities such as the late Princess Diana and made a name for himself in the Paris fashion scene. His dream was to start a new venture that would change the way men dressed in thobes *(traditional male apparel). His theory was that the* thobe *had not changed in hundreds of years, and everybody dressed and looked the same, making no fashion statement whatsoever. He wanted to develop men's fashion in a very conservative society. That seemed almost impossible to many, but Yahya did not think so. One of his major breakthroughs in the market was dressing the late King Abdullah when he was crown prince. That was a major icebreaker, after which everyone followed suit. Within a few years, Yahya had managed to change the way most Saudis dressed, young to old.*

Later, many other designers imitated him, and some achieved fame that has probably exceeded his. One of the most successful is Lomar, a male clothing designer brand which developed and overtook the market with its youthful designs and multiple outlets. Even though Yahya got nothing for his IP of the newly designed thobe, he said he was happy to have "opened the door" for the fashion design industry in Saudi Arabia, and indeed he had. As an artist, he never attempted to protect his breakthrough. Hundreds of young men and women are now proud to call themselves "fashion designers," something they could not have done if it was not for Yahya. He gave this industry a good image in a society that had not accepted it, or even understood it, a few years earlier. However, this new industry started producing new monopolies of its own. The newcomers started producing cheap designs in China for different segments of society. Cheap production began to dominate the market. For years, Yahya resisted industrializing his business into mass production, wanting to be a haute couture designer only. But with time, lack of protection, and an understanding of society's limited appreciation of high quality, he joined the boat of mass production (but, as he puts it, "without compromising quality"). Recently, he has released a new line of children's clothing, while keeping his adult line haute couture. Yahya is an example of a smart businessman who knows how to steer the boat to adapt to market changes. He is also a great example of someone who beat the monopolists once, by creating a new market, and was able to join them when it suited his interests.

 RELATED TIPS: 38, 40, 46, 59

Chapter 5

Financing Your Startup

Finance, to any organization, and startups in particular, is a necessity, as water and air to living beings. I have mentioned at the beginning of each chapter the suitable type of finance for each phase of a startup, and will explain in this chapter each one of them in detail. We will also explain several bootstrapping techniques, and positioning your startup properly for finance.

Generally, there are two types of finance: *debit* and *equity*. Under debit finance goes bank loans, letters of credit, and all bank financing types, while selling part of the company to finance some of its operations is considered *equity finance*. Angel investment, venture capital, and private equity are all equity finance schemes.

Monetary instruments such as mortgages, bonds, and Islamic *sukuk* maybe a little advanced for startups; however, convertible notes, which are a monetary instrument, are widely used in the venture capital community.

Finally, Appendix 5 includes an infographic that visualizes all types of startup finances in KSA.

Which seed would you like, watermelon or cucumber?

Your financing source will depend on the life stage of your venture. Position your startup for investment before you seek funding.

Before applying for funding, define what stage you are at. Do you have an idea requiring seed money? Are you looking to grow and expand, looking for a buyer, or launching an IPO (initial public offering)? An early startup that has not made enough income to sustain its existence, or has not even started generating income, requires seed money. Later-stage startups are the ones that are looking to grow and expand their business and have managed to secure considerable traction and income. Based on the stage your startup is in, you can seek the following stages of funding, in order: seed capital, angel investment, micro-VC financing, venture capital financing (series A, series B, series C...etc.), mezzanine financing and bridge loans, and finally, IPO. (Please refer to the infographic in Appendix 5.)

Many startups don't know who to approach and waste their time knocking on the wrong doors. Knowing where you are helps you narrow down which investors you should be approaching. Each startup stage requires a different set of investors. Many of the tips in this book help you identify different types of investors you should be looking at when you are looking for funding. The debate over whether to invest in a business plan or not goes on. It is true that some business plans may be too detailed, and obsolete by the time they are read. However, VCs will want to look at some document, even if it is short. Having a solid business plan eliminates that excuse from your rejection letter.

Venture capitalists speak "venture financial" and need the entrepreneurs to learn the language first. Saudi

Arabia has billions in venture finance almost untapped, and hundreds of entrepreneurs dying to get funding. The reason is that VCs mostly look at expansion- and growth-stage ventures, at a minimum investment of $0.5 million–$1 million in Saudi, and $10 million–$15 million in the USA. Entrepreneurs, on the other hand, are either too lazy to learn "venture finance lingo," too small for VCs, have not reached the VC funding stage, or are simply not ready. If you can't afford a document written by a top financial house, at least make sure you have a professionally prepared document or PPM (check Tip 82) showing all the numbers VCs want to see, calculated in a professional way. If they see potential in your business, they will make the effort to investigate it more. But what they will rarely do is write the document or do the calculation for you. Angel investors and seed funds, unlike VCs, are rarely interested in a detailed business plan. They are more interested in you, your product, and your potential. They take a less structured approach to identifying opportunity. However, as stated in related tips, getting a valuation is in your favor, and can help protect your rights. It is less of a formal requirement and more of protection for you.

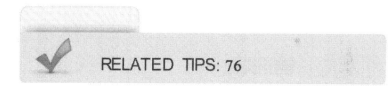

RELATED TIPS: 76

We found the fool from FFF. Shall we ask him for investment?

FFF (friends, fools, and family) are the first source of investment for most startups. You are not making a break out of the norm if you follow this route.

All of us have turned to friends and family for help at certain points in our lives when times got tough. Some try to take money from an unsuspecting fool. This category of people is coined "FFF." If you are turning to them for help, you are not alone. FFF is one of the main sources of funding for early-stage startups.

When new entrepreneurs hear the media hype about seeds, angels, VCs, micro-VCs, and financing, they often get the wrong impression that they can apply to any of these for funding. Well, that's true to an extent, but depending on the stage of the venture (as you will see in related tips), different types of financing apply. Once you move beyond the idea stage and start having some elements of a business, your destination should be an angel investment. Angels invest in startups before they start making money, which is something VCs rarely or never do. FFF is classified as a type of angel funding. (Check Appendix 5.)

When I started my very first business, all I had was an idea for a specialized consulting business that was not offered by consulting houses in Saudi Arabia. I did not exactly approach an angel investor, because I did not know he was one. He was an acquaintance who offered me a job, which I refused. When I told him that the reason for turning his offer down was that I wanted to start my own business, he liked the idea and offered me a partnership. This put him under the FFF category. Before that, I had made several attempts to partner with people that I knew, who were already more familiar with the market. My driver was to find a value investor, who helped me carry the cost of startup, introduced me to the relevant businessmen, and helped me get our first set of deals. By a few years later, I was able to land as many deals as he did, because I had built a name for our startup. Most entrepreneurs have a story similar to mine: they get their first support from someone who believes in their abilities and invests only out of that belief, and not necessarily based on a sophisticated business plan. Hence the name "angel."

RELATED TIPS: 71, 73, 75, 76

For many early-stage startups, grants, seed fund programs, and competitions can be a substantial source of funding.

When you only have an idea or a prototype for a product, it's hard to get funding from angels or micro-VCs, let alone from VCs. As I explain in related tips, these types of investors look at companies who have made initial traction and have some income. If you don't want to join an accelerator program, don't get admitted, or don't like their terms, there are a few other sources for funding available to you.

Business plan competitions work with many entrepreneurs who have only ideas, and not necessarily a working product. Of course, you will compete with hundreds of others, but if you win, you may get $100K of funding, or even more. Seed funds are also a good source for early-stage startups. Seed funds are usually run by governments and universities with the aim of helping startups. Grants for startups are also provided by government programs in many countries.

KAUST (King Abdullah University for Science and Technology) runs one of the few seed fund programs in the region. It offers both students and outside applicants the chance to receive a $200K grant. The only condition is that the sponsored businesses have to work with one of KAUST's staff and give the university a share of the IP, if any. One of the companies that managed to use this grant money to create and fund its app is Visual Experience, who launched the app Makkah Navigator, mentioned in the example of Tip 11. The two founders of Visual Experience joined forces with a German PhD student at KAUST, who helped them develop the code for the augmented reality application. The founders were natives *of Makkah who wanted to preserve the historical sites demolished under the Grand Mosque expansion project. The team of three provided value and covered the technical and marketing aspects for the app. The application allows you to see the destroyed sites by hovering on where they used to exist. It also displays historical descriptions of the main historical sites in and around the Grand Mosque when an iPhone or an iPad is pointed at them.*

 RELATED TIPS: 71, 72, 75, 76

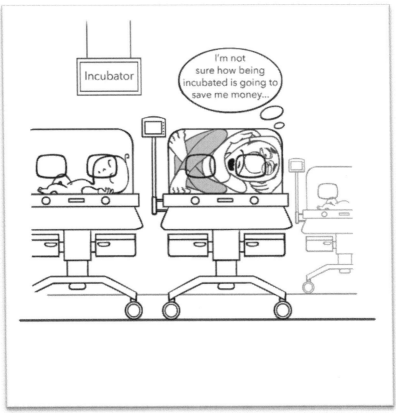

Avoiding the Valley of Death, part 1: Get your startup incubated. You will save money from free office space, services, and utilities.

Ninety percent of startups fail, and most of them do so in the "Valley of Death." This is the stage during and after validation when you are trying to make sales to sustain your business. Many startups in the idea stage find that there is nowhere to go but to an incubator. In order to win real investment, you need more than a paper idea. A prototype is the least you will need to provide to an investor to win their trust, unless you have a proven track record that convinces them to trust your scribbles.

Moving into an incubator can also help save you money until your project starts gaining traction and either makes money or qualifies for an investor. For an early-stage venture, utilities, rent, and services are very expensive and can wind up costing money that is badly needed elsewhere, for validation, launch of the product prototype, or marketing.

When I started BASE Consulting in 1994, there were no incubators in Saudi Arabia. But if there had been, it would have been wise for me to get incubated to save on rent and utilities. What we did instead was the closest available thing to incubation: we shared office space with another company, by renting out half of our office to another startup. We saved on rent, but we still paid for phone, electricity, very expensive dial-up Internet, and half the rent of a relatively expensive apartment. We had to buy our own furniture and equipment. Later, we got a large project with a major industrial group that owned a failing IT company. Our task was to run that company, identify its problems, and fix them. The project was significantly bigger than we were, as the company we were fixing had ten times more staff than we did. As a result, part of the deal we worked out was that we would move closer to their ailing company, by setting up shop in a building owned by the industrial group. This allowed our incubation to continue in an indirect way. The money we saved was significant for a small startup. If you get incubated, you will get rent, utilities, and shared services for free. Companies leave an incubator either when they get an investor or get enough sales to sustain their existence. Those who fail in both cannot stay incubated forever.

RELATED TIPS: 78, 79

No one mentioned paying bills when we did the Silicon Valley tour.

Accelerators can be great options for startups. If you are willing to give up equity for their services, join one.

Incubators and accelerators are great ways to get lots of services for free or against a minor stake in your company. An incubator, as described in the previous tip , is usually funded by a government program, and rarely asks for any type of equity. However, they pay no cash. Accelerators, which are mostly privately owned and run, give you all that an incubator provides, in addition to mentoring and access to potential investors, against equity of 5–10%. They also pay you $10K–$30K in cash. They take that risk on you hoping they can make money when an investor joins and buys part of your and their shares in later rounds of financing.

Many entrepreneurs are afraid of giving up any shares in the beginning. However, as the reader will see in this book, it is almost inevitable that you will have a partner at some point in time. Accelerators not only harbor you, but also try to find an investor for you. Being more professional and connected than you, they are likely to make better decisions about investors than you. In addition, it is in their interest to make the best choice, since their main aim is to maximize the value of their shares in your startup.

Many countries offer incubators funded by the government. There are many in the USA, Europe, MENA, and particularly in Saudi Arabia. According to the Saudi business incubator network, there are thirty-six incubators in Saudi Arabia alone.[67] Accelerators are new to MENA, but they do exist. Most follow the model of Y Combinator, the number one accelerator in the USA. Y Combinator is

---

[67] http://www.sbin.org.sa/en/default.aspx

where Dropbox and Reddit graduated. The program is offered a few times a year, lasting for two to three months. They offer direct funding between $14K and $20K, depending on the number of founders, and take 6% equity. In Saudi Arabia, the Ministry of Labor supported the start of the first accelerator, Flat6Labs. They take 15–20% equity and offer $15K–$20K. The home office of Flat6Labs is in Egypt. Jordan, Lebanon, and the UAE have similar accelerators.

 RELATED TIPS: 71, 74

Do you have any collateral other than this e-mail from the brother of the late African king?

Common myth: banks and venture capital groups fund startups. In fact, banks never do this, and VCs only rarely fund early-stage ventures.

Many entrepreneurs need to seek funding at the very early stages of their venture because of their own lack of means. Many of them feel that they should be getting this funding from banks, and express great dismay with the fact that banks rarely look at them seriously. They may feel that they are at a disadvantage because of the country they are in, or because of their type of venture. The truth is that banks will only lend money when they are almost certain they will get it back. If you, as an entrepreneur, are not sure when or if the money will come back, then how can the bank be sure? After all, it is other people's money they are lending you.

VCs are not that different. It's true that they work with startups and high-growth ventures, but at a later stage. VCs, by their nature, look to invest in ventures with proven business models that have already made profits. VCs pour money into ventures to help them achieve higher returns or scale up. This method of investment means that VCs typically work with large amounts of cash, up to a $1 billion under management. As a result, they don't spend a lot of time looking at ventures requiring funding of less than $10 million–$15 million dollars. In the US, seed-stage companies received only 3% of allocated VC funds in 2012.[68] The other 97% went to more mature startups.

In the late '90s, I started looking for funding beyond my angel investors to help finance the business operations for IFS Arabia (which later joined the Alcantara

[68] *National Venture Capital Association Yearbook.* (New York: Thomson Reuters, 2013), p. 27.

group). I started off by contacting banks in Saudi Arabia. Banks in that country are very conservative, and this is as true today as it was fifteen years ago. They prefer to fund large corporations where the risk is lower. They also look at funding with large amounts of cash in order to make more profit. I remember talking to all eleven of the banks operating in the country at the time, and all of them required high collaterals. Most of them asked for a cash guarantee of 100%, or even 110%, which seemed ridiculous to me. We needed to build a credit history with them before they would fund us more. When we got our first bank loan for Alcantara Group in 2007, ten years after we started petitioning, it was a line of credit in excess of $3 million. The bank asked for guarantees that added up to 400%: the signing off of proceeds in full of one of our major contracts with the government, 200% of partner stocks, and the personal assets guarantee of the partners. Once we paid off our first debt, they started reducing the collateral. Most startups will die before reaching that point.

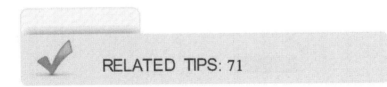

RELATED TIPS: 71

...As a cost-cutting measure, we will eliminate phones, computers, and e-mails and introduce the iCan communication system.

Bootstrapping is one method to finance your startup when you lack other outside finances. Sources can be supplier, customer, employee, and general admin expense reductions.

Bootstrapping is a metaphorical phrase that means "depending on yourself for financing." No VCs, no banks, no angels, nothing. Sometimes this plan is really just like it sounds, trying to use your own bootstraps to pull yourself up—i.e., impossible. But if you plan it well, you may get away with it.

You have expenses and income in your financial statement. Go back and check the expenses one by one and see how you can save money on each one. Employees need to get paid, unless they are (partially) compensated by something other than cash, such as share options or a percentage of profits. Suppliers may be willing to wait on their payments if you give them more money or if you accept less than the offered discount for their goods. Customers might consider paying you earlier if you offer them more services, more goods, or some sort of discount. The related tips cover some of these options in greater details.

One of the great bootstrapping techniques I used to get cash for my startups was to sell company debts to my partners. Back in the 2000s and before IFS Arabia hit it big, we needed cash to support our expenses until we got paid by our suppliers. As mentioned in the related tips, we could never get a reasonable loan from the banks. So I did two things. First, I offered my partners a deal to support the purchase of certain goods with interest. In Islamic finance, this is called murabaha. *I borrowed an agreement from one of the local banks that offered such loans for cars and houses. I adjusted the terms of the agreement to reflect our business and offered it to my partners. For them, injecting more cash was not attractive. But offering them an investment that paid 10% in a year was great, and better than anything an investment bank could offer. I know 10% sounds steep, but it's better than using a credit card, and the best deal I could get. My second method was to approach my largest customers, who paid us annual maintenance. I offered to let them pay for two years instead of one at a 7% discount. They loved the idea. Now I finally had enough cash reserves to run my operations. I also got back at the banks indirectly, which made me very happy. The example in Tip 76 helps explain why.*

RELATED TIPS: 76, 78, 79

Avoiding the Valley of Death, part 2: Get one customer on board. They may demand harsh concessions from your side, but they will help test the product, and cover part of your expenses.

A new startup is hungry for cash. But not all cash has to come from investors or loans. Every investor that comes in will dilute your shares. The more investors you have, in single or multiple rounds, the less you will own of your own company. Taking out personal loans against your assets to finance your business shows commitment, but it can also be dangerous and can leave you penniless.

One of the great bootstrapping techniques is to get one customer on board early on. Generally, such a transaction is known in Islamic finance as a *salam* sale. This first customer is in it to take advantage of you against the risk they are taking with your product. But that's fine; give them favorable terms, better prices than the market leader, and more time. In return, you will sell your first product for a very valuable first reference. Additionally, you will get to test your product in real life for free, and you will get very valuable cash that is drawn against neither equity nor your personal assets.

In the summer of 2013, two young entrepreneurs from an aspiring new startup came to my office with a medical referral app. One of the founders had quit his job and put all his life savings into creating the startup. He told me that he had even delayed his marriage plans to make this work. He had a niche for his product, and although his business model had not been tested in Saudi Arabia, where he intended to launch it, it was successful worldwide. There are a few successful similar apps in the US. He was selling seats for around $200/month to each doctor's practice. His business proposition was to save young doctors time and money on full-time referral and *booking staff. However, he did not have enough traction or enough doctors. In order to get doctors on board, he needed a large number of downloads, and to get the downloads, he needed a large number of doctors. Catch 22!*

I hooked them up with a group of clinics that already had a hundred doctors and two hundred thousand patients and were looking to develop their own app. The clinics refused to pay him $200 per doctor, but agreed to pay him much less. My advice was to take the deal for at least a year. Not only would it give them income, but it would also provide free product testing and allow the entrepreneurs to grow their traction exponentially. Later, they could adjust their fees upward from a better position. This jump-start to the business was of high value to them, since it would cost them thousands of dollars of operational and marketing expenses if they attempted to grow their venture organically. The entrepreneurs, unfortunately, had doubts and held out for further negotiation. Eventually, the clinics have decided to simply develop their own app, as they already have the infrastructure to support it. The entrepreneurs', unfortunately, have abandoned their project and stopped working on it.

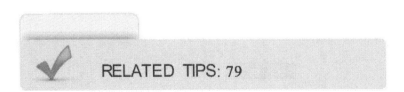

RELATED TIPS: 79

Avoiding the Valley of Death, part 3: sign an off-take agreement or a joint venture between your startup and a customer. Guaranteed sales are cashable.

Off-take agreements are one of the common ways to avoid the Valley of Death as explained in the last tip.

Another way to avoid cash problems is to partner with your customer either as an equity shareholder or in the form of a joint venture between your startup and their company. The joint venture can guarantee cash for you while you buy and produce for them. The downside of both techniques is that it may hinder your freedom to work with other customers whom your partner competes with. They will also know some details of your operations you may not want to share, and have a board seat in your startup, giving them some form of control.

A great classic example of this is how Bill Gates sold DOS to IBM. IBM had never written an operating system before, so Gates pointed them toward an OS written by Gary Kildall. The OS was CP/M, which had sold around six hundred thousand copies. However, when IBM could not reach an agreement with Kildall, they asked Gates to develop an OS for them for $50K (some say $75K). Microsoft developed the OS for IBM in six weeks, and the rest is history. I should point out that DOS was named after the original QDOS, which is an abbreviation for Quick and Dirty Operating System! This is a term used by developers when they develop something quick, ignoring software engineering and lengthy quality measures, which require more time for development. That product and that agreement helped Microsoft become what it is today. The size of that deal was relatively small, but Gates knew that having IBM as a customer could make Microsoft products as popular as the IBM PC. And *it did. Had Gates started to become greedy, or refused like Kildall, Microsoft would probably not have made it, or died like CP/M, which lost the chance to lead the market and change history. It's also worth noting, however, that Microsoft itself did not develop DOS. It outsourced it to Tim Paterson, who worked for Seattle Computer Products. The deal between Microsoft and IBM was kept secret from Paterson, who felt betrayed and was bitter at Microsoft, but that's another story.* [69]

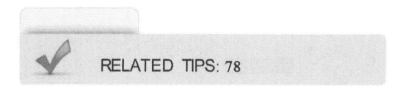

RELATED TIPS: 78

[69] *They Made America: From the Steam Engine to the Search.* Harold Evans, with Gail Buckland, and David Lefer New York: Little, Brown, and Company. 2004. pp.411–412. "Engine: Two Centuries of Innovators."

...I will invest your next year's salary in the company with 0.5% returns, which I will donate on your behalf to the company's CSR program.

Bootstrapping techniques startups should never use: delaying employee salaries and supplier payments beyond due dates.

An unfortunately common strategy of small businesses in Saudi Arabia is to use the staff payroll for bootstrapping even if the company has cash. Some business newcomers, and a bunch of established ventures, let their cash grow so thin that they can't afford to pay staff salaries, nor suppliers.

Stories of staff salaries delayed up to six months are not uncommon, especially in labor-intensive companies. The usual excuse is the delay of contractor payments. A working capital finance agreement with a bank can solve this problem, although small businesses can't afford or may not be qualified for such an agreement, as I have mentioned in related tips. The recently introduced "wage protection program" aims to end the practice of staff payment delay permanently. It allows the Ministry of Labor to monitor whether companies are paying staff salaries on time or not. This program has started to be applied to small businesses only in 2017.

Sometimes the head of a company is forced to make a choice between two necessities: paying his suppliers or paying his own staff. The trick is trying to balance the two, because both are equally important. One of the first Internet service providers (ISPs) in the Kingdom went bust because the GM chose to pay his staff on time every month but ignored his suppliers. I'm not sure whether he conducted a full review of his HR (human resources) costs in an attempt to avoid the disaster, but his policy ended up killing the company. After a year of delaying supplier payments in anticipation of payments from subscribers, in an extreme volatile environment, where laws and regulations were being changed, the company faced a grim reality. It had accumulated enough debts that the owners decided not only to fire the GM, but also to close the business. The business model for ISPs changed that year, and user distribution became automatic depending on the zone the users dialed up from.

Many contractors, particularly in operations and maintenance, delay staff salaries. This has caused, on more than one occasion, their staff to stop working; the delay in productivity that this results in impacts public services negatively. Many of these companies have a bad reputation and may never get business from the government again. The fact that their contractor payments were delayed is not an acceptable excuse. If you are going into a labor-intensive business, make sure that your business model covers prolonged delays in your payments.

 RELATED TIPS: 62

Focus on sales, and investors will come to you; focus on the investors' money, and you will lose both.

Many entrepreneurs are finding the right financiers because of poor relationships. In contrast, a handful of showprenuers have been attending investors' conferences, exploiting their knowledge and adversely affecting the rest. The permanent presence in the media and conferences scene has been exploited to fool investors that they are successful company owners, in order to obtain frequent funding while neglecting the development of the company's performance, selling power, and expansion. They invent fictitious success stories and travel from stage to stage, and from prize to prize. They have no business experience except prizes and stories of struggle at the beginning of a business, if you can call designing logos and printing business cards a struggle. Real entrepreneurs spend most of their time selling. Thus, investors may be neglected to the extent that it is difficult for them to move the company to the next stage, so the balance between the two is very important.

The emergence of the breed of showprenuers hurt the rest of the serious entrepreneurs, as it has lowered some investors' confidence in the entrepreneurs and the seriousness of their projects. For example, there is a story about an "entrepreneur" who left a startup and the whole country for a scholarship after receiving funding, and another spent the funds on furniture and other things not related to the essence of the business. Some of these practices, because of the lack of numbers in both parties, have made the market more difficult for everyone in recent times. A veteran investor cannot invest without "due diligence." However, some of these companies may be offering new ideas or are in the initial stages, making the investor venture without examination.

The way to the pocket of the investor is not by providing offers with resonance or prizes, or by obtaining media coverage. These things may give you the opportunity to meet investors, but if you do not have an attractive record of sales and growth, they will not initiate anything. What most investors are looking at is initial sales, market reaction, and scalability. Investors want a return on their money and will not be able to turn leading images on magazine covers or prizes into returns that support their investment portfolio.

One of the young entrepreneurs won a famous award in 2014 and received extensive media coverage. He then got a contract to be incubated by Badir. But instead of taking advantage of his new fame to support his sales, increase his experience, and improve his business model, he took advantage of that opportunity to get another round of investment. The young man came to me two years later while working on a venture capital fund and asked for funding.

When I performed a due diligence examination, I realized that his sales equated to zero. He did not even take advantage of the funds from the awards and funding to develop his sales. Instead, he spent it partially on the development of the product, and developed features that weren't in demand by the market. The rest of the award money was spent on himself and his partner—making it seem more like an award for deceiving their investors—in

295

apparent disregard for the investors. Even his office in the incubator was vacant, because the "entrepreneur" himself was a full-time employee and did not give the startup any interest other than the media presence. After I rejected him, other investors realized he was completely neglecting his company, and ignored him. If he had focused on sales, he would not have been asking to be financed, and perhaps investors would have knocked on his door without much effort from his side.

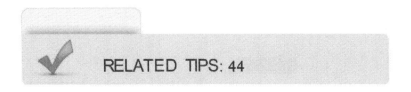

RELATED TIPS: 44

Can you teach me investor "tackling" techniques?

Approaching investors requires specific techniques. Get advice before you approach them. You may not get a second chance.

Many entrepreneurs know they want an investment and exert big efforts in trying to find one. But once they land a meeting, their tongues get tied and they don't know what to say. As we have repeatedly mentioned in related tips, considering a meeting with an investor requires learning a new language other than your native "techie" tongue. You either have to learn to speak it or get a translator to do it. Investors speak "venture financial," and if you have not learned the basics, please don't go.

The good news is that learning "venture financial" is not rocket science, and you can easily master it. If not, you can get professional assistance to help you put forward a great presentation and produce a financial document. You have to be able to answer basic questions about your business financials as confidently as you can talk about your system features and your apps' technical superiority. The investor is mainly interested in how much money you want for how much equity, for how much of a return, and how soon. All their questions lead to these basic questions, one way or the other. In the early stages, you may be able to get away with no business plan. But as your business gets bigger, professional documents become a necessity you can't avoid.

Most young entrepreneurs learn the grim reality that they don't speak "venture financial" when they first pitch in front of an investor. I recall the first time I tried to do so in 2002. I was ready to talk about our business and how it had grown by 500% in five years, but I had no valuation, no IRR figures, and no five-year projections, and my presentation was lengthy and boring. After I got that first, "No thank you," I hired a financial consultant to help me prepare for the next one and draft my very first private placement manuscript (PPM). It cost some money, but it was well worth it. It was not only a service I outsourced, but also a training course in investor-speak. As mentioned in related tips, most venture capital firms complain about entrepreneurs not having the right tools to assess their own business.

RELATED TIPS: 26, 71, 83

Investing in an expensive valuation does not guarantee an acquisition at that value, nor does it stop your buyer from doing their own due diligence.

When you get to the stage where you are looking at serious investments, beyond FFF and angels, you will be asked for full financials, including audited statements for three to five years back, and a formal valuation or a PPM, which would also include five-year projections, among much more information about your business. A formal valuation is a document written in "venture financial," the language you had to learn. These documents must be written by a specialized financial house to be credible. Usually, VCs and high-net-worth investors ask that you provide them with a formal valuation. When they do, they expect this valuation to be from a star financial house.

Even though you will spend an arm and a leg getting a formal valuation, which can cost from $100K to $500K depending on which country and which firm is performing the valuation,[70] this valuation only serves as a benchmark, and it will not guarantee that you will receive the valued amount for your business. An investor always does his own due diligence. This means they will look into your business and try to come up with another number, usually lower than the number your expensive manuscript suggested. You have to learn to accept this, and work on negotiating with your potential investors. The investor will seek to find means to challenge your valuation. He will only ever pay less, and you can never ask for more. Your expensive valuation will serve as a ceiling for what you can request.

---

[70] Cost in Saudi Arabia averages between $20K and $80K, and maybe less in some MENA countries.

Back in 2010, we hired Saudi Hollandi Capital (now Alawwal Capital), one of the few licensed financial houses in Saudi Arabia, to evaluate Alcantara group. We did extensive digging through our books to provide them with everything they needed. Their job was to look at our five-year projections and challenge every number. They also looked into the past ten years, our historical sales, customer relations, supplier relations, partnerships, and pretty much everything that had to do with the business. In the end, they used a mixture of many valuation methods and came up with three different valuations and an average. When we first went pitching, the investor we met with challenged even the lower number. All subsequent investors did so as well. The document, however, served as a credible source to initiate the negotiations. Negotiating for investment is a hard and a painful process, and its outcome is not predictable. Deals may give you money, or they may provide cash injections only and no take-home money for you. Term sheets can pretty much be anything—they may offer conditions, convertible loans, clawback clauses, even clauses that can get us fully diluted at future funding rounds, and all sorts of tricks. VCs and investors are usually savvy in such games, and they will take advantage of entrepreneurs' inexperience. The best thing for you to do is get really good advice when negotiating a deal.

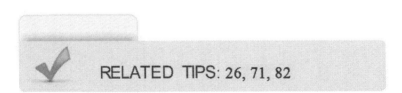

RELATED TIPS: 26, 71, 82

Even if you offer me 2 cents a share, I'm not giving up more than 5% of my startup equity.

Don't hold on to startup shares worth very little. A value-added investor may make your new share worth far more than your old 100% ownership.

A new startup is hungry for cash. But not all cash has to come from investors or loans. Every time an investor comes in, they will dilute your shares. The more investors you have, the less you will own of your own company. There is a thin line between being greedy— holding on to 100% of nothing—and being stupid: letting go of your brainchild in full to a greedy investor.

Part of being smart is knowing when to let go and who to let go to. When you get an opportunity to partner with a real value-added partner, take that chance and negotiate hard (but not so hard as to scare them away!). Always remember that holding on to 100% of your $10 company is like holding onto 1% of a $1,000 company as an example. Everyone has partners, and you are no different if you do. Cash infusions can shortcut you to a point where it would take you years to arrive at organically, if you ever did.

Partnerships can help grow your company or make you lose it. A strategic partner at the right time can help you grow beyond what you can do on your own. When I started my first company, I needed a partner. I was new to business and knew virtually no one in Saudi Arabia, and I needed someone to show me the ins and outs and guarantee some customers to kick off the business. Three years later, I sold a company I bought against debt for three times its buying cost. The person we sold it to took us to another level with his group companies. Having these two partners reduced my shares in my business from 100% to 50% to 30% over time. But the value of my share increased by three-digit multiples in 2010. This happened in part because of the value those partners were able to add. Had I stayed with my 100% shares of my original $6K investment, I probably would have taken much longer to get to the 1,000x mark. In all these companies, I was still the person running the business and was the face of the enterprise. Sure, I reported to a board, but as we've mentioned in related tips, who doesn't have a boss? The example from Tip 46 with Uturn is a good example of smart entrepreneurs who gave up 51% of their company to a very valuable investor. Without him, they never would have grown by 1,500% in just three years and never would have gotten the multimillion-dollar investment after years of hard work eventually.

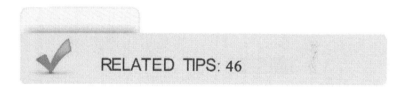

RELATED TIPS: 46

The CEO is busy: He's backing up his thoughts to the cloud.

For many startups, acquisition, rather than an IPO, has become the target. Many companies are determined from the outset to get acquired by one of today's giants.

Before the dot-com bubble burst, it was almost a rush to get publicly listed. The market did not understand IT properly and was dazzled by the instant success of a few companies such as Yahoo, AOL, Netscape, and other startups of the time. Companies with virtually no history got investors and were publicly listed. Once the bubble burst, the market regained its senses and judged all companies by their sales and profitability once again. However, even today, when you get a billion users, like on Facebook, this huge traction is factored in, as we have seen in the past year or so. Facebook was released at $38 a share, which initially went down but then picked up again by leveraging its huge user base. Eventually, the company broke its original $38 benchmark. Twitter, which at the time had no profits yet, was listed in the New York Stock Exchange for $26 a share. Its share prices flew up by 72% on the first day of trading, before settling down at a lower price, but higher than the IPO price. The market price for Twitter, just like Facebook, is based on the speculation of potential sales to its hundreds of millions of active subscribers.

Nowadays, a lot of companies know that if they pose a real threat to one of the market players, they will be acquired by them. This process has evolved to the point that it has become almost a business model for some companies, to work on getting acquired by focusing on a niche that can skim off a giant's clientele enough to cause a potential threat. The micro-VC business model almost relies on having companies in their portfolio acquired as opposed to being publicly listed.

A recent example of that is Instagram. The application provided functionality that Facebook lacked, and allowed its users to do simple alterations and share their photos on Facebook quickly from their smartphones. Facebook, realizing that smartphone users were its potential future, did not want to take the risk of competing with an app that was already successful in an arena it was still developing. That eventually led Facebook to acquire them for almost $1 billion. For the same reason, Amazon acquired Souq, a competitor in the Middle East market. Acquisition to Amazon was better than entering a war with Souq. It also means instant acquisition of a customer base, experienced staff, and assets. Noun, in contrast, a newcomer to the MENA e-commerce market with deep pockets, failed to do this. It entered the negotiation around the same time as Amazon and lost in the end.[71]

Rocket Internet, as we discussed in related tips, has made it their business to create a threat by copying business models. Many times its strategy has led to acquisition, after numerous failed lawsuits. Many micro-VCs and VC firms today advertise the companies they hold in their portfolios on their websites. If a company had been acquired, usually by one of the big companies, it would proudly announce this fact. Check out this quote from Felicis Venture's website: "Since 2006, we have invested in over ninety companies, forty-seven of which have been acquired by industry leaders such as Apple, AT&T, Disney, eBay, Facebook, Google, Groupon, Intuit, Microsoft, and

---

[71] Giles Turner and Selina Wang: "Amazon Buys Souq.com as Middle East Online Market Takes Off," March 28, 2017. www.bloomborg.com//news/.

Twitter."[72] Note that Felicis does not list an IPO. Many others don't either. This is how things are nowadays.

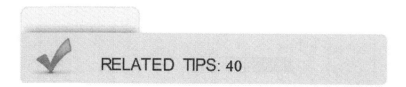

RELATED TIPS: 40

---

[72] www.felcis.com

About the Author

Khalid Suleimani is an accomplished venture capitalist, angel investor, and serial entrepreneur, with over twenty-five years of experience. He's the Chairman of the Board of Wadi Makkah Ventures, a Wadi Makkah Company, and also sits on Wadi Makkah holding board and the investment committee of Iktifaa Charity Co.

Some highlights of his career include successfully starting, growing, and exiting four out of seven companies, as well as structuring several VCs. Khalid also restructured Sirb (the leading Saudi angel investor network backed by KACST) and served as its president between 2014 and 2017. His achievements include executing digital transformation projects and computer system implementations for over fifty private, public, military, and government entities.

The Arabic version of this book became a MENA Best Seller Entrepreneurship book, and it was reprinted six times. This second edition is issued in parallel with the Arabic sixth edition. Khalid has held numerous public engagements and startup judging events. Khalid holds a master's degree in electrical and computer engineering from the University of Colorado, an executive education certificate on launching new ventures from Harvard Business School, and a certificate from a venture capital program by Investeurope. He holds a CME-1 certificate from the CMA and is a certified consultant by both MOCI and the Saudi Council of Engineers.

Mr. Suleimani grew up in Sheffield, England. However, he returned with his family to Saudi Arabia after completing the fifth grade. In his twenties, he relocated to Boulder, Colorado, for higher education, where he earned his master's degree in electrical and computer engineering. He started his PhD studies around the same time he created his first startup. After publishing two papers on visual programming and passing his PhD qualifying exams at CU Boulder, he took a break to create his second startup. A year later, he dropped out of the PhD program to focus on his entrepreneurial career.

Appendix 1

MORAN, STAHL & BOYER INTERNATIONAL
900 28th Street
Boulder, Colorado 80303
303 449-8440
303 449-1064 (FAX)

Celebrating 20 Years of Intercultural Service

June 1, 1993

To Whom It May Concern:

Mr. Khaled Suleiman worked for Moran, Stahl & Boyer as a cross-cultural consultant for our training programs on Saudi Arabia in 1993. Our business is international cross-cultural training and consulting. This requires that we have multidimensional, talented and worldly people. Mr. Suleiman's role as consultant for MS&B is to help understand, identify and explore important cultural differences between our clients' culture and that of Saudi Arabia.

I would like to share some of the comments that our clients have made:
"Very good. Open and frank exchange. Extremely enlightening."

"Fantastic! Khaled was the highlight of our training. His openness and frankness along with his extensive experience was wonderful."

"Khaled was outstanding. He deserves special praise. Open, honest and most informative."

"Khaled was invaluable to the program. So open and honest - never hesitated to answer any question. I learned so much from him."

We have very much enjoyed working with Mr. Suleiman; he was an asset to our program as the comments reflect above. He is a true interculturalist and will be missed by MS&B.

Sincerely,

Karen Hamady

Karen Hamady
Program Coordinator
Training Department

A Unit of Prudential Relocation Management International Division

Appendix 2

Helmi Kutbi Road Statistics (tip 12)

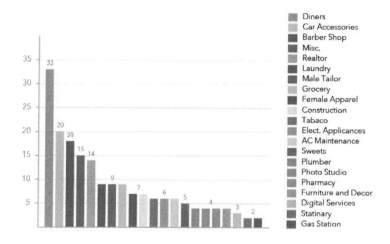

- Diners
- Car Accessories
- Barber Shop
- Misc.
- Realtor
- Laundry
- Male Tailor
- Grocery
- Female Apparel
- Construction
- Tabaco
- Elect. Applicances
- AC Maintenance
- Sweets
- Plumber
- Photo Studio
- Pharmacy
- Furniture and Decor
- Digital Services
- Statinary
- Gas Station

Helmi Kutbi Road Map

Appendix 3

A typical scenario for establishing a startup

Step	Duration	Fees	Hidden Charges	Comments
1 Registering Startup name	one day	0	none	
2 Automatic registration of startup as a co	instant	2,400.00	none	two years min
3 Electronic declaration of registration	instant	600	none	
4 Registration with justice department	one day	0	none	Physical presence required
5 Chamber of commerce Registration	instant	4,000,00	none	two years min
Total Ministry of commerece fees		7,000		Unified invoice issued
6 Civil defence Approval		150	5,000	75/SQM For less than 100 Sq meters area, and SR 150/SQM for larger areas plus Fire extinguisher and lighting required
7 Municiplaity license	three to six months	300	40,000	While problem was solved for office business with shared co working spaces, shopes still have to pay rent until licensed
8 Office sign with 2 SQM area		400	none	Municipality Requirement
total Municipality fees		850	45,000	
9 Wasil Postal adress registration	one day	500		Required for MOL registration
10 Registering in Labour Office	one day	0		Requires municpal registration
11 GOSI Registration	instant	0		Requires for MOL registration
12 Total Staff Registration costs		500		
13 DZIT registration and paying taxes		1,250	7,000	Auditor fees required to pay taxes
Total		9,800	52,000	
Grand Total for all registration requirements		61,800		
Government Fees for second year				
1 GOSI Registration		30,000,00		Five staff members with average pay for GOSI+ 1% for Sanid 9% 5000
2 Assuming profits of SR 50K		1250	7000	via auditor 2.5%
3 Fees Refund program for new companies		-8350		Applies to all companies less than 3 years old
Total Operational fees		29,900		
Grand total for first two years		91,500		Required by regulation not including any operational expenses

Assumptions:

3 enterpnuers decided to establish a startup with totally local staff, and went on to register their online startup which should generate 2 more jobs contributing a total of 5 jobs to the economy

314

Appendix 4

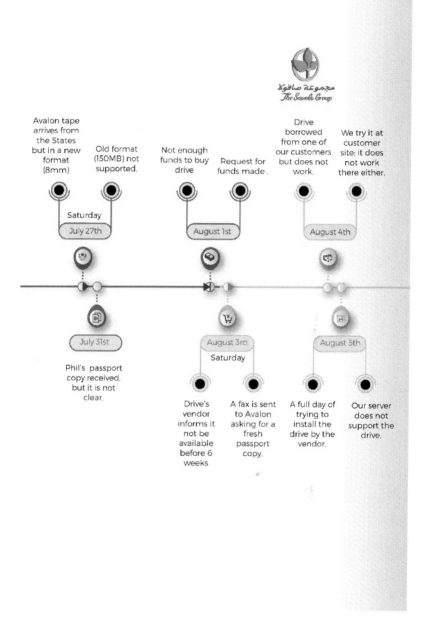

Avalon tape arrives from the States but in a new format (8mm)

Old format (150MB) not supported.

Not enough funds to buy drive

Request for funds made .

Drive borrowed from one of our customers but does not work.

We try it at customer site; it does not work there either.

Saturday
July 27th

August 1st

August 4th

July 31st

Phil's passport copy received, but it is not clear.

August 3rd
Saturday

August 5th

Drive's vendor informs it not be available before 6 weeks

A fax is sent to Avalon asking for a fresh passport copy.

A full day of trying to install the drive by the vendor.

Our server does not support the drive.

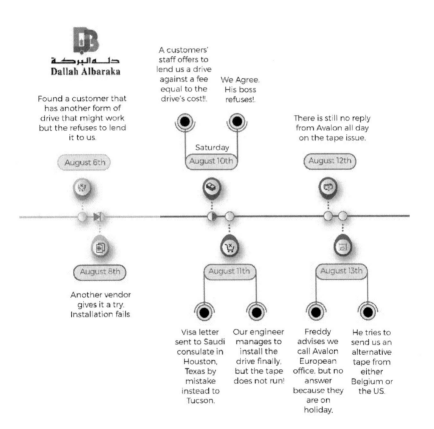

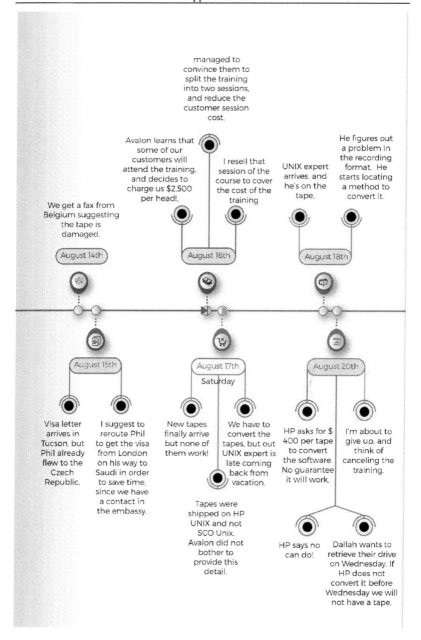

managed to convince them to split the training into two sessions, and reduce the customer session cost.

Avalon learns that some of our customers will attend the training, and decides to charge us $2,500 per head!.

I resell that session of the course to cover the cost of the training

UNIX expert arrives, and he's on the tape.

He figures out a problem in the recording format. He starts locating a method to convert it.

We get a fax from Belgium suggesting the tape is damaged.

August 14th

August 16th

August 18th

August 15th

August 17th
Saturday

August 20th

Visa letter arrives in Tucson, but Phil already flew to the Czech Republic.

I suggest to reroute Phil to get the visa from London on his way to Saudi in order to save time, since we have a contact in the embassy.

New tapes finally arrive but none of them work!

We have to convert the tapes, but out UNIX expert is late coming back from vacation.

HP asks for $ 400 per tape to convert the software. No guarantee it will work.

I'm about to give up, and think of canceling the training.

Tapes were shipped on HP UNIX and not SCO Unix. Avalon did not bother to provide this detail.

HP says no can do!

Dallah wants to retrieve their drive on Wednesday. If HP does not convert it before Wednesday we will not have a tape.

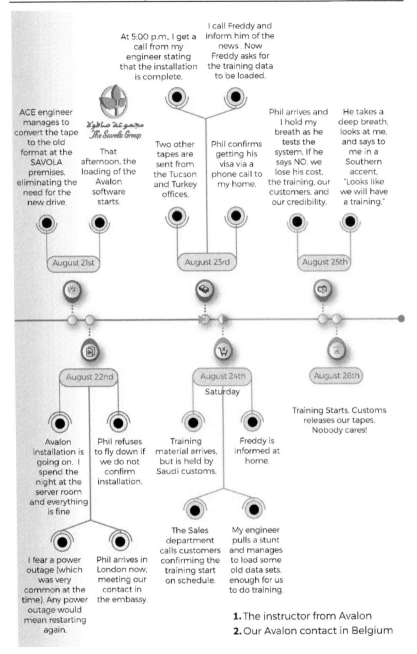

At 5:00 p.m., I get a call from my engineer stating that the installation is complete.

I call Freddy and inform him of the news . Now Freddy asks for the training data to be loaded.

ACE engineer manages to convert the tape to the old format at the SAVOLA premises, eliminating the need for the new drive.

The Savola Group

That afternoon, the loading of the Avalon software starts.

Two other tapes are sent from the Tucson and Turkey offices.

Phil confirms getting his visa via a phone call to my home.

Phil arrives and I hold my breath as he tests the system. If he says NO, we lose his cost, the training, our customers, and our credibility.

He takes a deep breath, looks at me, and says to me in a Southern accent, "Looks like we will have a training."

August 21st

August 23rd

August 25th

August 22nd

August 24th
Saturday

August 26th

Avalon installation is going on. I spend the night at the server room and everything is fine

Phil refuses to fly down if we do not confirm installation.

Training material arrives, but is held by Saudi customs.

Freddy is informed at home.

Training Starts. Customs releases our tapes. Nobody cares!

I fear a power outage (which was very common at the time). Any power outage would mean restarting again.

Phil arrives in London now, meeting our contact in the embassy.

The Sales department calls customers confirming the training start on schedule.

My engineer pulls a stunt to load some old data sets. enough for us to do training.

1. The instructor from Avalon
2. Our Avalon contact in Belgium

Appendix 5

Active VC funds in KSA as per startup lifecycle stages

Photos

"Launching New Ventures" executive education program graduates, Harvard Business School, Boston, 2013 (Intro).

Alcantara corporate Team, Jeddah office, 2010. (Tip 23)

Sirb fifth pitching event, Jeddah, 2018. (Tip 5)

With President Clinton SFG100 award ceremony, Riyadh 2011. (Tip 36)

Chief executives of Ericsson and Saab visit to IFS Arabia Jeddah offices 2004. (Tip 50)

Receiving an Award from Deputy minister of defense, Riyadh 2007. (Tip 52)

Swedish Trade delegation to the Kingdom Headed by HRH Princess Victoria, Jeddah 2004. (Tip 50)

With Dr. Ingo Behrendt , CEO Nexus A.G, at the Saudi e-health summit, Riyadh 2008. (Tip 69)

Printed in Poland
by Amazon Fulfillment
Poland Sp. z o.o., Wrocław